Dr**o**p

DE**A**D

Drop Dead

DEAD

A Horrible History of
Hanging in Canada

Lorna Poplak

DUNDURN
TORONTO

Cover image: Noose: istock.com/Owat Tasai
Printer: Webcom

Library and Archives Canada Cataloguing in Publication

Poplak, Lorna, author
    Drop dead : a horrible history of hanging in Canada / Lorna Poplak.

Includes bibliographical references and index.
Issued in print and electronic formats.
ISBN 978-1-4597-3822-5 (softcover).--ISBN 978-1-4597-3823-2 (PDF).
--ISBN 978-1-4597-3824-9 (EPUB)

    1. Hanging--Canada--History. I. Title.

HV8579.P67 2017   364.660971   C2017-902308-X
                                          C2017-902309-8

1 2 3 4 5   21 20 19 18 17

We acknowledge the support of the **Canada Council for the Arts**, which last year invested $153 million to bring the arts to Canadians throughout the country, and the **Ontario Arts Council** for our publishing program. We also acknowledge the financial support of the **Government of Ontario**, through the **Ontario Book Publishing Tax Credit** and the **Ontario Media Development Corporation**, and the **Government of Canada**.

Nous remercions le **Conseil des arts du Canada** de son soutien. L'an dernier, le Conseil a investi 153 millions de dollars pour mettre de l'art dans la vie des Canadiennes et des Canadiens de tout le pays.

Care has been taken to trace the ownership of copyright material used in this book. The author and the publisher welcome any information enabling them to rectify any references or credits in subsequent editions.
— *J. Kirk Howard, President*

The publisher is not responsible for websites or their content unless they are owned by the publisher.

Printed and bound in Canada.

VISIT US AT

dundurn.com | @dundurnpress | dundurnpress | dundurnpress

Dundurn
3 Church Street, Suite 500
Toronto, Ontario, Canada
M5E 1M2

For my family

CONTENTS

Murder is unique in that it abolishes the party it injures, so that society has to take the place of the victim and on his behalf demand restitution or grant forgiveness; it is the one crime in which society has a direct interest.

— W.H. AUDEN, from "The Guilty Vicarage: Notes on the Detective Story, by an Addict," published in *Harper's Magazine*, May 1948

AUTHOR'S NOTE

For the names of people and places in this book, I have generally followed the spelling found in *Persons Sentenced to Death in Canada, 1867–1976: An Inventory of Case Files in the Fonds of the Department of Justice*, Government Archives Division, National Archives of Canada, 1994. I do deviate from this rule, however, when other reputable sources point to a different option.

Another word on spelling: John Robert Radclive was a prominent Canadian hangman in the late 1800s and early 1900s. Some sources give his last name as Radcliffe or Ratcliff, but the name is spelled Radclive in this book.

The terms "gaol" and "jail" are variants of the same word, signifying a prison for the detention of people awaiting trial or with sentences of less than two years. Whether a specific prison is named a gaol or a jail depends on generally accepted usage: for example, Ottawa has its Carleton County Gaol as opposed to Toronto's Don Jail.

I plowed through many statutes and other government documents in my search for materials for this book. Fortunately, I came across a medley of more exciting sources as well. Archival newspapers, for one. In earlier times, both before and after the advent of newer media such as radio and television, people depended on print media, particularly newspapers, for reports on local and world events. These papers, many of which are now available online, serve as a mine of information for modern researchers. Tucked into the reams of virtual newsprint, I found glittering nuggets of information, such as the description of a notorious hangman who snored like a "traction engine" the night before a hanging, or the fact that an axe killer was possibly insane but generally all right, except when he had been drinking, or the poignant details of a condemned person's last meal. I am also hugely indebted to the wealth of secondary sources — books, articles, and visual and audio materials — I consulted in my efforts to provide a nuanced view of the people, places, and events that featured in the history of hanging in Canada.

INTRODUCTION

The condemned man clutched the wooden handrail of the prisoner's box, waiting for his sentence.

The judge was wearing a black cap and black gloves when he swept back into the courtroom. Slowly and deliberately, he sat down at the bench and began to read: "Prisoner at the Bar, it becomes my painful duty to pass the final sentence of the law upon you. You have been found guilty of murder. You will be taken from here to the place whence you came and there be hanged by the neck until you are dead, and may God have mercy on your soul."

Death by hanging — a long-standing Canadian tradition.

Capital punishment, the execution of someone found guilty of a crime, dates back to the arrival of European explorers on our shores. In those days, if you were condemned to death, quite a wide range of methods could be used to punish you. You could be hanged, or face a firing squad, or be burned at the stake. You might even be put to death by a multiplicity of methods. For example, just after the first proper settlement was established in Quebec City in 1608, explorer Samuel de Champlain learned that a locksmith named Jean Duval was conspiring to kill him. Duval was arrested, found guilty, hanged, and strangled. Then his head was cut off and stuck on a pike on the highest rooftop of the fort, as "food for birds," according to the nineteenth-century American historian

Samuel de Champlain, explorer, cartographer, and administrator of the colony of Quebec. Originally taken as authentic, this image was later found to be a false portrait, based on a 1654 engraving of Michel Particelli d'Emery.

Francis Parkman — a stark warning to other settlers who might be considering similar schemes. The display was also meant to serve as a stern message to the local Indigenous peoples that the newcomers meant business.

In 1763, the conclusion of the Seven Years' War, the first global conflict in history, saw Britain and her allies victorious and France defeated. Large swaths of previously French-owned mainland North America, including Quebec, fell under the sovereignty of Britain. Although Canada remained a collection of separate British colonies until Confederation in 1867, a Royal Proclamation in 1763 replaced the prevailing Canadian legal system with the laws of England.

Within the criminal justice system, the British strongly favoured hanging for the punishment of capital crimes, preferably in a marketplace or similarly busy area to ensure a large audience. Why hanging? Historically, other methods were used, such as beheading for high-born folk or burning at the stake for heretics. But traditionally, the most common form of capital punishment since Saxon times was hanging. The thinking was that, even without optional extras like beheading, hanging was a pretty nasty sentence, well befitting felons found guilty of heinous crimes. By the end of the 1700s in Britain, however, the litany of crimes regarded as sufficiently horrible to warrant the death penalty had swelled to 220, including such nefarious acts as keeping company with gypsies or skulking in the dark with a blackened face.

In Canada, too, public hangings based on the English model gradually became the only method of dealing with serious crimes. As in Britain, the list was long: in the early 1800s, people were sentenced to death by hanging for more than a hundred different offences. Fraud and burglary were on the list. Two men, N. Ganson and A. Jeffreys, were hanged in 1821 for passing forged bills. In 1828, Patrick Burgan of Saint John, New Brunswick, aged eighteen or nineteen, received the death penalty for the double offence of stealing a watch and some money from his former employer and clothing from a sailors' boarding house. Given the power and pre-eminence of religion in Canada at that time, your very life would have been in jeopardy if you were caught scrawling slogans on the side of a church. You could also be hanged for stealing your neighbour's cow, which was the fate of B. Clement of Montreal. And just in case you thought that the law protected the young as it does today, think again. Children were regarded as miniature adults and treated as such — Clement was only thirteen years old when executed.

In 1859, the catalogue of crimes in the statutes of the United Province of Canada (Ontario and Quebec today) was reduced to a more manageable number. On the list were "murder, rape, treason, administering poison or wounding with intent to commit murder, unlawfully abusing a girl under ten, buggery with man or beast, robbery with wounding, burglary with assault, arson, casting away a ship, and exhibiting a false signal endangering a ship."

By 1865, the number of capital crimes had been pared down further. Out went buggery and burglary and arson; from then on, only murder, rape, and treason were punishable by death.

July 1, 1867, marked the date of Confederation: precisely at noon, the two new provinces of Ontario and Quebec, together with New

Brunswick and Nova Scotia, joined to form the Dominion of Canada, with John A. Macdonald as its first prime minister.

By 1905, a uniform criminal code had been rolled out to the Northwest Territories, Yukon Territory, British Columbia, Alberta, Saskatchewan, Manitoba, and Prince Edward Island as they all folded into the Dominion. Newfoundland was a latecomer in 1949. Nunavut, the newest territory, was carved out of the existing Northwest Territories in 1999, more than twenty years after capital punishment was abolished.

According to the official inventory of Department of Justice capital case files, over the course of the 109 years from Confederation until 1976, when the death penalty for civil (as opposed to military) crimes was removed from Canadian law books, 704 people were hanged, 11 of them women, and all but one of them for murder. Louis Riel, the Métis leader from Manitoba who launched two rebellions against the Canadian government in the late 1800s, was the lone exception. He was executed for high treason.

This horrible history of hanging in Canada will focus on the period between Confederation and the abolition of the death penalty. It is a story of murder (and one treason) and hanging. It begins with a double slaying in St-Zéphirin, Quebec, and effectively ends in 1962 with a double execution in Toronto, Ontario, although another fourteen years would elapse before capital punishment was finally abolished.

You will meet men, women, and children, those who were hanged and those who escaped the noose. You will meet judges and jurors and police officers and farmers and hookers and gangsters and ghosts. Above all, you will encounter the hangman and find out how he was affected by his job. You will be introduced to the science and art of hanging, and you will see what can happen when things go terribly wrong.

Hanging was a harsh reality during the first century after the Confederation of Canada. Does the topic still have relevance today, or is it a dark chapter best relegated to the faded annals of our past?

Some crimes are so horrific that a life sentence doesn't seem adequate. Consider Canadian serial killers Clifford Olson, Paul Bernardo, and Russell Williams. In each case, a call was made for the return of the death penalty. Canada's last hangman, John Ellis, was a firm believer in capital punishment. And even though the death penalty was eliminated in Canada more than forty years ago, a 2013 poll found that 63 percent of Canadians still agreed with him.

Could we — should we — reinstate the death penalty?

At the end of this history, you be the judge.

CHAPTER 1

Celebrating Confederation:
Three Hangings in the First Year

Modiste Villebrun and Sophie Boisclair were desperately in love. The burly lumberjack and his paramour yearned to spend the rest of their lives together. There was just one problem. They were both married — to other people. What were they to do? They lived in the small, conservative French Catholic community of St-Zéphirin, Quebec. In 1867, divorce would have been inconceivable. The church saw to that. They just *had* to come up with another strategy.

They chose murder.

The first results seemed quite promising. Granted, there were some whispers in the community when Villebrun's wife, who had reportedly been in excellent health just a few days earlier, died suddenly. The gossip came to nothing, and the lovers were emboldened to press on. Things changed radically, however, when Boisclair's husband, François-Xavier Jutras, died soon after. To the plotters' great misfortune, Jutras had fallen acutely ill on a few occasions prior to his death. Suffering from convulsions and abdominal and neck pains, he consulted a doctor. The physician became very, very suspicious when his patient died. An autopsy showed that Jutras's demise had been caused by strychnine poisoning.

The lovers were accused of murdering Jutras. They were tried separately, each of them by judge and twelve-man jury, in the nearby town of

Sorel. By this time, people were paying a lot more attention to Villebrun and Boisclair's goings-on. As the Crown attorney said in his opening address at Villebrun's trial: "There is no doubt that the two accused committed the crime of adultery. It does not necessarily follow that a person who forgets God's commandment 'Thou shalt not commit adultery' will forget the one that says 'Thou shalt not kill,' but when you are on the downward slope of vice, you do not know where you will end up."

The trial took ten days, but the jury needed only five minutes to find Villebrun guilty of murder. And the only possible sentence was death by hanging.

Then it was Boisclair's turn. She, too, was found guilty, but before the judge could pronounce her penalty, she dropped a bombshell.

"Sir," she told the clerk of the court, "I do not want the sentence of death to be delivered at the present time, because I am pregnant." Sure enough, as was customary, a specially convened jury of married women and a court-appointed doctor examined her and confirmed her pregnancy.

As Jeffrey Pfeifer and Kenneth Leyton-Brown point out in *Death by Rope: An Anthology of Canadian Executions*, the two murderers should have been executed together, which might have led to a reprieve for both of them until after the child was born. In the end, Villebrun's execution went ahead as planned, and on May 3, 1867, he was led to the scaffold alone. Ten thousand people turned up at his public execution. In a weird twist, Boisclair also witnessed the event, albeit reluctantly. The window of her cell overlooked the square where the gallows had been set up.

The British parliament passed the *British North America Act* creating the Dominion of Canada in March 1867. Even though this execution took place two months before actual Confederation, it is, somewhat confusingly, officially listed as the first hanging in the new nation.

Boisclair escaped the noose. When her baby was born several months later, her sentence was commuted to life imprisonment on the recommendation of the minister of justice. She was locked away for twenty years in the Kingston Penitentiary in Ontario.

Sophie Boisclair was described by a surgeon as "of unsound mind" when she was finally released into the care of her son in 1887. Time has

Department of Justice handwritten memorandum about Sophie Boisclair's status prior to her release from the Kingston Penitentiary in 1887. It describes her as having been of unsound mind for a number of years.

fogged so many details of these early cases, but how tempting it is to speculate that this was the same child whose birth had rescued her from the gallows in 1867.

Ethan "Saxey" Allen was an ex-convict originally from Detroit, Michigan. The *Detroit Post* described him as "a hard character … always found with bad associates" and "rather notorious as a rough and a gambler." He became the leader of a four-man gang that robbed banks and plundered businesses along the Canadian shore of Lake Ontario, always one step ahead of the frustrated police.

The Allen Gang's luck ran out in the early hours of September 22, 1867; so did that of Cornelius Driscoll. Driscoll, employed for twenty-four years at the Morton Brewery and Distillery in Kingston, Ontario, had started working as their night watchman just two weeks previously.

The gang broke into Morton's with sledgehammers and crowbars in search of $2,500, which they knew was locked away in the safe. When Driscoll came to investigate the noise, Allen killed him with a sledge-hammer. Early the following morning, a local resident found the dead man lying in the distillery yard, and the hunt was on. The gang members fled with their loot, but they were tracked down and arrested in a hotel in Watertown, New York.

The criminals were brought back to Kingston and tried at the Frontenac County Court House. Allen was convicted of murder, although the jury added a recommendation for mercy. The judge did not share the jurors' merciful sentiments, informing Allen that he held out no hope for pardon. Two of Allen's accomplices got nine- and ten-year sentences in the Kingston Penitentiary for manslaughter.

The *Detroit Post* said at the time that the murder "was one of the most cold blooded and brutal affairs of the kind on record," but it does look as though Allen had a change of heart before he went to the gallows at the Frontenac County Gaol behind the courthouse on December 11. Asked by the sheriff if he had anything to say, he replied: "No, nothing at all. Only I hope that my fate will be a warning to others." He refused to have the customary black hood (called a "cap") pulled over his head and,

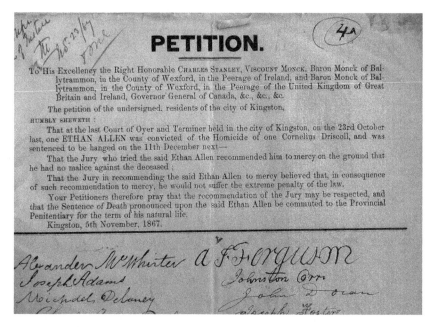

PETITION.

To His Excellency the Right Honorable CHARLES STANLEY, VISCOUNT MONCK, Baron Monck of Ballytrammon, in the County of Wexford, in the Peerage of Ireland, and Baron Monck of Ballytrammon, in the County of Wexford, in the Peerage of the United Kingdom of Great Britain and Ireland, Governor General of Canada, &c., &c., &c.

The petition of the undersigned, residents of the city of Kingston,

HUMBLY SHEWETH :

That at the last Court of Oyer and Terminer held in the city of Kingston, on the 23rd October last, one ETHAN ALLEN was convicted of the Homicide of one Cornelius Driscoll, and was sentenced to be hanged on the 11th December next—

That the Jury who tried the said Ethan Allen recommended him to mercy on the ground that he had no malice against the deceased ;

That the Jury in recommending the said Ethan Allen to mercy believed that, in consequence of such recommendation to mercy, he would not suffer the extreme penalty of the law.

Your Petitioners therefore pray that the recommendation of the Jury may be respected, and that the Sentence of Death pronounced upon the said Ethan Allen be commuted to the Provincial Penitentiary for the term of his natural life.

Kingston, 5th November, 1867.

On November 5, 1867, the citizens of Kingston submitted a petition requesting that Ethan Allen's death sentence be commuted to life imprisonment. The petition was denied. On December 11, Allen was hanged at the Frontenac County Gaol.

as the hangman pulled the bolt, he said "Lord, have mercy on me," before dropping to his death.

Legend tells of a ghost that stalked the Morton Brewery and Distillery for many years thereafter. The spirit of Cornelius Driscoll, the watchman who was bludgeoned to death on that September night in 1867, continued to patrol the hallways, checking all the locks.

Dominion Day, July 1, 1868 — a special holiday declared by Governor General Lord Monck to celebrate Canada's first birthday. Just imagine everyone's excitement when the day finally dawned. There were picnics and parades and speeches and twenty-one-gun salutes and splendid bonfires and even torchlight processions after dark.

The city of St-Hyacinthe, Quebec, came up with a very odd way to celebrate this momentous anniversary: to wit, Canada's third public hanging. A crowd of about eight thousand men, women, and children gathered around a scaffold set up in front of the jail. Onlookers gasped with horror and pity and women fainted as the condemned man, Joseph Ruel, was half carried, half dragged to the scaffold.

He took seventeen minutes to die.

The *Montreal Gazette* said the next day that "the execution naturally threw all St-Hyacinthe into sadness, and was a damper to all enjoyment of the national holiday."

As with Modiste Villebrun, love was the undoing of Joseph Ruel.

He was having a passionate and rather public affair with Arzalie Messier, the wife of a farmer named Toussaint Boulet: witnesses at Ruel's trial claimed to have seen the couple embracing and grappling on several occasions. Under the pretense of helping Boulet with his treatment for what seems to have been a sexually transmitted disease (probably syphilis), Ruel started to feed the farmer a cocktail of poisons. Ruel made the mistake of obtaining these substances (arsenic and strychnine) from local doctors, ostensibly to deal with pesky dogs and foxes. As Ruel had not professed any previous interest in trapping foxes, the authorities became suspicious when Boulet died. The police concluded that he had been poisoned and Ruel was charged with murder.

Arzalie Messier was not charged. As noted by historian Ken Leyton-Brown in *The Practice of Execution in Canada*, this may have reflected the community's sympathy toward a woman who had been wronged by her husband. Toussaint Boulet's disease was seen as proof that he was a sinner who had destroyed his marriage. He had been unfaithful to his wife for a long period, and his risky sexual behaviour endangered her life as well as his own.

But the courts would not tolerate murder. Ruel had poisoned Boulet. The jury found him guilty, with no recommendation of mercy. In sentencing Ruel, the judge criticized him sharply for robbing the victim of both his wife and his life. Ruel was hanged less than two months later.

Remember Saxey Allen's words as he went to the gallows? "I hope that my fate will be a warning to others."

That is exactly what the lawmakers and politicians and medical professionals and large numbers of the general public wanted to hear. They hoped — no, believed — that the fear and horror of a death by hanging would deter others from committing heinous crimes.

This deterrent effect worked in two ways, they argued. First, if the punishment were severe enough, it would discourage criminals from perpetrating further monstrous acts. In legal terms, this is referred to as "specific deterrence" and is not really relevant to the capital punishment debate. After all, dead men commit no crimes. Second and more important is the idea of "general deterrence." This view holds that potential murderers would think twice — or many times — before copying the behaviour of a hanged criminal. And if, after all that, you *did* go ahead and murder someone — well, then, it was all your own fault if you found yourself hanging by your neck from the gallows.

But there were other lawmakers, politicians, medical professionals, and members of the public who questioned that view. Before Confederation, the prospect of being hanged hadn't prevented people from committing even minor offences like stealing a cow or a horse, so how could the death penalty be regarded as effective at all?

Once the deterrent effect of hanging came into doubt, other uncomfortable questions arose. Was the only principle underlying capital punishment that of retribution — punishment for wrongdoing — or, even more unsettling, simple biblical-style revenge: "an eye for an eye and a tooth for a tooth"? Some claimed that the punishment should fit the crime, and that the execution of murderers was justified, especially when the victim was a policeman or a prison guard, the true protectors of our society. Others, like the late, great Canadian defence lawyer Edward Greenspan, argued that "the real reason why this barbarous practice persists in a so-called civilized world is that people still hold the primitive belief that the taking of one human life can be atoned for by taking another."

The naysayers pointed to other problems, too. People might go to the gallows simply because they had a tough prosecutor or an inadequate defence lawyer — if they had one at all. This was very clearly illustrated in the case of Elizabeth Workman of Mooretown, Ontario, who was arrested for murdering her husband, James, in October 1872. Scott M. Gaffield notes in "Justice Not Done: The Hanging of Elizabeth Workman" that when Elizabeth's trial opened on March 20, 1873, it became clear that she had neither a lawyer nor the means to hire one. As a result, the court asked a local barrister, thirty-three-year-old John A. Mackenzie, to handle her case. The trial started the next day, leaving Mackenzie mere hours to familiarize himself with the facts and formulate a defence in this life-and-death battle. All he could come up with was a statement of Elizabeth's innocence. He neither questioned nor challenged witnesses during the two-day trial, nor did he make reference to the good character of his client or the fact that she was more than likely the victim of spousal brutality. As future prime minister Alexander Mackenzie (no relative of lawyer John A.) argued in a letter in May 1873, "there was no opportunity of bringing out evidence that might tilt in her favour. The unfortunate woman had no counsel engaged, and no one interested in assisting her." And as for the counsel who was eventually appointed, "what could he do on a few hours' notice?"

There were yet more troubling questions that emerged in the pro- and anti-capital punishment debate. What if something went horribly wrong during the hanging; for example, if it took too long for someone to die, as had happened to Joseph Ruel?

And, most disturbing of all, what if, by some dreadful mistake, the wrong person went to the gallows?

CHAPTER 2

The Deadly Game of Hangman

In March 1902, Stanislaus Lacroix was executed in Hull, Quebec, after murdering his wife and a neighbour. A rare photo shows the condemned man standing on the trap door beneath a gallows. His arms are pinioned with black straps, and a cap is draped over his head. The noose dangles down beside him. Gathered around are four men. Two priests in their cassocks and the sheriff with his cocked hat, gown, and sword stand to his right. And on the left, the same side as the noose, the hangman waits, dressed in a dark suit and white shirt. Three other officials — doctors, perhaps? — are at the bottom of the scaffold. Two of them look up toward the doomed man. Within moments, the trap would be sprung and Lacroix, as described in the *Ottawa Citizen*, would be "dashed to eternity."

But many other individuals were involved in the game of Hangman in Canada before that final grim act took place. Unlike the vaguely grisly children's guessing game, real Hangman truly was a matter of life and death. If you were convicted of murder, there was one, and only one, sentence available — hanging.

The game began with a death, and 704 times in Canada's first century, it ended with a death, too.

So before we get too far ahead, let's meet some of the principal players whose specialized roles made them stand out from the rest.

The execution of Stanislaus Lacroix in Hull, Quebec, March 21, 1902.

First, there had to be a body: spread-eagled on a city street, slumped over a desk, buried in a shallow grave in field or forest. Even in the one and only case where the convicted man, Louis Riel, was hanged for high treason and not for murder, there was a body. Thomas Scott, a troublesome adventurer from Ontario, was court-martialled and executed by a Métis firing squad during the Red River Rebellion in Manitoba in 1870. Blame for his death was laid squarely on Riel and played into Riel's own trial and execution some fifteen years later.

The ink was scarcely dry on the *British North America Act* that established the Dominion of Canada in 1867 when Official Murder Victim Number One, François-Xavier Jutras, a farmer in St-Zéphirin, Quebec, met his end by strychnine poison. The very last murder victim, killed in a hail of hammer blows just before capital punishment was abolished in 1976, was Georges Nadeau, a thirty-four-year-old paint-shop instructor at the Cowansville Penitentiary, Quebec.

For every victim, there has to be an aggressor — a man, woman, or child who pulls the trigger or plunges the knife or slips arsenic into a cup of tea. Nadeau's nemesis was French-Canadian Mario Gauthier, just nineteen years old. Gauthier became one of the last eleven men ever to spend time on death row in Canada. By that time, death sentences were routinely being commuted to less severe punishments, but in his case, it wasn't necessary. The Court of Appeal granted him a new trial, and he was allowed to plead guilty to manslaughter. He ended up being sentenced to eleven years for his crime.

When Mary Lane of Brandon, Manitoba, a pregnant mother of four children, was shot at close range on the afternoon of July 5, 1899, suspicion initially fell on a tramp with a foreign accent. The vagrant had come to the Lane residence and had shot Mary when his request for food was refused. Or so said Emily Hilda Blake, the Lanes' twenty-one-year-old domestic servant, who had arrived in Canada from Britain as an orphan some ten years previously. The city was in an uproar over the news, but within four days, the real perpetrator was in custody. It was Blake herself. Police investigations revealed that she had purchased the gun used in the shooting. Once confronted with the evidence against her, she confessed.

The youngest individual ever convicted of murder (and hanged) in post-Confederation Canada was sixteen-year-old Archibald McLean. Archie was the most junior member of the Kamloops Outlaws, a gang of four Métis youths who caused chaos in the Fort Kamloops area of British Columbia in the late 1870s. The desperadoes kicked off their life of crime with robbery. As quoted by Hamar Foster in his essay on the Kamloops bandits, one neighbour complained, "This is a fine state of things, to be terrorized by four brats who have threatened to burn the jail in order to destroy the records of their deeds." The so-called brats moved on to horse rustling, then to murder. Archie shot at point-blank range the Hudson Bay Company's Fort Kamloops representative, John Ussher, who was generally in charge of law and order in the settlement. Ussher had led a poorly armed posse to the outlaws' camp in search of a stolen stallion. The gang followed up that murder with the random killing of a sheep herder, on the unlikely pretext that the man had drawn a gun on them. A much larger, better armed, and very angry posse flushed them out of the cabin where they had taken refuge, threatening to burn them out if they didn't surrender. The youths were locked up in the Kamloops jail pending their trial at New Westminster, British Columbia.

With the accused in custody, the official tasked with organizing the trial was the local sheriff. But if you think of a sheriff as a dude in the Wild West walking down a dusty road with a shiny star on his chest, spurs clanking on his heels, and a pair of six-shooters on his hips, think again. That archetype did not live in Canada. Agreed, the Criminal Code defines sheriffs as "peace officers." The official Service Canada website adds that "sheriffs execute and enforce court orders, warrants and writs, participate in seizure and sale of property and perform courtroom and other related duties."

While some Canadian sheriffs in earlier times and in smaller centres might have been rough-and-ready types, others were more like Ernest Charles Drury, farmer, writer, and premier of Ontario from 1919 to 1923. After his fall from power, Drury spent a few years dabbling in federal politics. In 1934, he was happy to be appointed sheriff, county court clerk, and local registrar of the Supreme Court for the County of Simcoe, Ontario — all for the "princely" salary of $3,750 a year.

Farmer, writer, and premier of Ontario Ernest Charles Drury, 1920. One of his duties as sheriff of Simcoe County, between 1934 and 1959, was to organize three murder trials.

As sheriff, Drury had a number of unpleasant "related duties" to contend with in the course of his twenty-five years on the job. Evicting tenants when they defaulted on their rent was one of them. Another was organizing three murder trials. He found the second of these particularly disturbing. In his memoirs, *Farmer Premier*, Drury described the prisoner as an "Indian boy" of about eighteen years. Without provocation, the youth had stabbed a friendly night watchman twenty-three times with a sharp piece of scrap metal snatched from a factory workbench.

Once the case went to trial and the action moved into a court of law, writes Ken Leyton-Brown, counsel for the Crown and the defence conducted interviews to choose the six- to twelve-member jury. Jurors were supposed to represent the public, but this was generally not the case. Women, or First Nations people for that matter, could be victims or murderers. But never jurors.

In court, the judge, invariably a man, became the most powerful player in the game. Inspiring fear and respect, he swept into the courtroom in his black robes at the beginning of a trial. Everyone rose, and he took his seat on a special raised platform, dominating the room.

Guided by the judge, the jury would weigh the evidence, decide whether the accused was guilty of murder beyond a reasonable doubt (or of the less serious crime of manslaughter, or not guilty), and deliver a verdict. Jurors played a supporting role right up to the dying moments of the trial, when the jury foreman stepped forward on their behalf to deliver his one and only speaking line: "Your Honour, we find the accused guilty as charged," or, for the lucky ones, "not guilty."

The jury's decision was most often driven by the judge's charge after all the evidence had been presented by the lawyers for the prosecution and the defence. This was an important step, notes Leyton-Brown, especially in difficult cases or where the law was complicated. The judge was generally very fair, but he sometimes made his opinions, positive or negative, crystal clear to the jury. In 1904, George William Gee of Woodstock, New Brunswick, was accused of murdering his young cousin and one-time girlfriend, Millie Gee, by shooting her twice in the side. In his review, a stern Chief Justice Tuck ordered the jury: "Don't, gentlemen, allow any mock sympathy to hinder you in rendering your verdict. Now go and do your duty." Are you surprised that the jury found Gee guilty?

As they usually knew that the accused would be hanged if found guilty, juries often struggled with returning this grim verdict. They sometimes hesitated to convict youths or people with families. Complicating this might be uncertainty about the identity of the perpetrator and scanty or largely circumstantial evidence — these and other factors made the jury leery of accepting someone's guilt beyond a reasonable doubt. When they felt particularly unsure, they exercised the option of recommending mercy. In one remarkable case in 1923 in Montmagny, Quebec, farmer Gustave Dubé was found guilty of shooting his wife. The jurors were horrified when they realized this meant the death penalty. They recanted, protesting that they thought the charge was manslaughter. Perhaps subscribing to the principle that ignorance of the law is no excuse, the judge refused to budge and Dubé went to the gallows.

As with modern cases, the judge's role was to decide whether evidence was admissible or inadmissible, interpret the law, and guide the jury's decisions. In capital cases prior to 1976, however, there was one notable addition. With a guilty verdict, the judge's final act was to deliver the death sentence. He would sweep out of the court, only to return immediately, to even more fear and respect, wearing a black cap upon his head and sometimes black gloves as well. As Leyton-Brown points out, these theatrics and rituals at the time of sentencing — cap, gloves, and the set wording of the death sentence itself — came to Canada, like most other court routines, courtesy of the mother country, Britain. They were all designed to underline the power and majesty of law and state.

Often the judge would lash out in his final address to the prisoner. In 1878, Michael Farrell, a violent man much feared in Ste-Catherine, Quebec, shot and killed a neighbour who was using a right-of-way through Farrell's property, in full view of the neighbour's children. As reported in the *Quebec Saturday Budget*, Justice Monk had this to say: "I cannot immagine [*sic*] how a man of your position and intelligence could possibly have conceived and carried out so terrible a crime. I will not recall to your recollection the horrible, sanguinary scene which took place, when you slew your victim in the presence of his little children and his friends, and slew him as you did, prisoner, without any provocation." According to the paper, Monk was very much more distressed than the condemned man, who sat calm and stone-faced throughout the judge's address.

Who would live and who would be condemned to death by judge and jury? The answer was often unpredictable. Take the opinion of Simcoe County's Sheriff Drury on two of the murder trials he oversaw. The first was the case of the eighteen-year-old Indigenous youth accused of stabbing a night watchman. The defence tried to prove that "he was mentally dull and perhaps retarded," but the judge and jury were hostile. The youth was sentenced to death, with no recommendation for mercy. The second case was that of two young men, also eighteen or nineteen years old, who shot, threw into a swamp, then shot again — this time to death — an older man who had made sexual advances to them. They were soon arrested and tried in Barrie, Ontario. The jury found them guilty of manslaughter, not murder, and the judge gave them less than the maximum sentence.

As Drury wrote of both cases in his memoirs:

> The savage nature of the young Indian's crime, which might reasonably have been taken to indicate mental instability and thus serve as an argument for clemency, quite evidently predisposed both judge and jury against the prisoner. I wonder if they had read stories of Indian massacres? In the second case, clearly a deliberate and cold-blooded murder, the youth of the prisoners, the squalor of their environment, and above all the existence of the death penalty, just as evidently predisposed judge and jury in their favour.

Once the trial was over, prisoners were generally sent to the local prison to await execution. They were segregated in a special section called death row and kept under constant surveillance. Although physically restricted, every condemned person was allowed unlimited access to a spiritual advisor, generally a Christian minister.

The minister taking care of the spiritual needs of inmates at the Don Jail in Toronto, Ontario, in the early 1960s was Salvation Army chaplain Cyril Everitt. "I will see you in heaven," Everitt said to Ronald Turpin and Arthur Lucas as the two men stood on the scaffold at the Don Jail just after midnight on December 11, 1962. Moments later, they dropped through the trap door together, the last ever to hang in Canada. In their final days on death row, as their appeals sputtered and died, Everitt visited them two or three times a day to cheer them up and pray with them. What was rare in this case, as Robert Hoshowsky points out in his book on Turpin and Lucas, *The Last to Die*, was Everitt's deep affection for his charges: he visited their graves for many years after they died.

The public, too, became invested in the spiritual well-being of prisoners on death row. The burning questions were: Would those doomed to die be redeemed? Would they in some way repent for the error of their ways? In religious terms, what society wanted more than anything was for evildoers to be saved from sin.

What society also desperately wanted was for evildoers to confess. As noted by Leyton-Brown, this would remove any last lingering doubt about whether justice had been done, or whether police, prosecutors, judges, jurors, and sheriffs had been complicit in sending an innocent person to the grave.

Best of all was repentance and confession together. Robert Neil, hanged in Toronto for the stabbing death of a prison guard, as reported in the *Toronto Daily Mail* on February 29, 1888, stood beneath the crossbeam of the gallows and said in a firm, clear voice, "Now I am here I would like to say I did not mean to kill that man.... I forgive everyone and hope to be forgiven." A rough arrow scratched on a wall at the Don Jail marked his grave.

Of course, things didn't always end as neatly as the public would have liked. Michael Farrell, the Quebecer found guilty of killing his neighbour in 1878 for using a right-of-way through his property, made a confession in court when sentence was passed: "That man had liberty as well as any other to pass by that road, as long as he fastened up the gap after him.... If he had put up the fence after him he would have been alive today, and I would not have been here." In reporting his words, the

Quebec Saturday Budget commented with horror and sadness on Farrell's "apparent unconcern and vindictiveness."

Government officials also had an essential role to play in deciding who should go to the gallows and who should be spared.

When someone was convicted of a capital crime, the presiding judge was required to submit a detailed report to the minister of justice in Ottawa. The federal Cabinet and officials of the Department of Justice would review the case. At the end of this sometimes lengthy process, Cabinet would make the ultimate decision on what sentence to impose. If they resolved that the law "be allowed to take its course," an Order-in-Council was issued instructing the local authorities to proceed with the execution.

According to author and historian Carolyn Strange, "condemned persons' chances of commutation were clearly linked to assumptions about the dangerousness of certain criminals and the culpability of various categories of offenders, as well as to public anxieties about changing rates of criminal violence." And what swayed the Cabinet's opinions at one time could have the opposite effect at another, tilting the balance for, or against, the condemned person. Indigenous peoples (that is, First Nations, Métis, and Inuit peoples), for example, were initially treated leniently, but as time passed, racial paternalism evaporated, especially if white people were in the gunsights.

Take the case of the Copper Inuit living on the shores of Coronation Gulf in the Arctic. In 1916, two Inuit men named Sinnisiak and Uluksuk were arrested for the murder of two French missionaries. They were initially tried in Edmonton in 1917 and acquitted, then retried in Calgary and convicted of murder. Their sentences were immediately commuted to life imprisonment. In 1919, the men were released and returned to the Arctic. This leniency was aimed to teach the Inuit people about Canadian law and to "Canadianize" them. If the Inuit were to kill again, they would have to suffer the consequences.

And the consequences proved to be harsh. In 1922, a young Inuit named Alikomiak, arrested with his uncle Tatamigana for the killing of an Inuit man and a baby, shot a Royal Canadian Mounted Police corporal whom he believed had insulted him. Later the same day, he shot a Hudson's Bay Company man.

Killing whites? Strategically acceptable to the Canadian authorities in 1917, but no longer tolerated in the 1920s. "As kindness has failed in the past I strongly recommend that the law should take its course and those Eskimos found guilty of murder should be hanged in a place where the natives will see and recognize the outcome of taking another life," thundered T.L. Cory, commissioner of the Northwest Territories.

In 1923, Alikomiak and Tatamigana were tried at Herschel Island in the Yukon Territory. Since trial court officials brought along with them an executioner and lumber to build a scaffold, it was fairly clear what the outcome of the case would be. Public controversy about the case spread across the country, with some arguing that it was a travesty of justice to try sixteen-year-old Alikomiak in a language he could not understand and others insisting that Canada's sovereignty should be maintained and respected. But despite this, the government was determined to make an example of the two Inuit men, and they were hanged in February 1924.

Not everyone convicted of murder went to the gallows, though. Just over half the 1,533 people listed in the official inventory of Department of Justice capital case files as having received the death penalty escaped the noose. In some cases, their sentence was commuted or quashed; in others, they were given a new trial leading to a reduced sentence or acquittal. Some prisoners awaiting execution died in jail. Chillingly, some unfortunates committed suicide.

So who was most likely to be executed? Statistics show us that certain groups of people, such as young working-class males and men from ethnic and racial minorities, were particularly vulnerable. The poor were often targeted. Women were generally treated leniently, as were Indigenous people in the early stages of their association with whites. However, racist thinking among the ruling classes would sometimes evoke pity for "lesser" peoples but at other times reflect fear and hatred of "the other." In short, there were never any guarantees, consistent application of the law, or immutable rules or principles in what Strange calls "the lottery of death" — capital punishment in Canada.

The main players are all assembled. Let's not forget the second-stringers, important in the action, too: police officers, homicide detectives, doctors, court officials, Crown prosecutors crossing swords with lawyers for the defence, jailers, and families of the victims and accused.

And standing by on the sidelines, waiting for his turn, is the most contentious participant of them all: the hangman.

The game is on.

CHAPTER 3

The Assassination of Thomas D'Arcy McGee: A Murder Mystery

Thomas D'Arcy McGee may have had a premonition that his brains would be blown out by an assassin's bullet. A few days before his death, he had a terrifying dream of tumbling into a powerful river and being swept helplessly toward a waterfall.

It was April 1868 and things had not been going well for McGee. Once a rising star among Irish Canadians, he had won a seat in parliament in the United Province of Canada (now Ontario and Quebec) in the general election of 1857 and had been instrumental in persuading Irish Canadians to support Confederation. But now his political career was in tatters. After playing a prominent role in the first two conferences in Charlottetown and Quebec that had led to Confederation, he was omitted from the third in London. He had been expelled from the St. Patrick's Society in Montreal and denounced as a traitor to Ireland. In spite of his waning political fortunes, however, he was elected by a slim majority to the first House of Commons in the Dominion of Canada in 1867. But the Cabinet position he had expected as a prominent member of the ruling Conservative Party did not materialize. His clashes with the Irish community made him a liability rather than an asset, and the proposal was withdrawn. Instead, he was offered a job in the civil service as a consolation prize.

But at 2:00 a.m. on April 7, 1868, all of this faded into the background. In the House of Commons in Ottawa, parliamentarians were on their feet, giving McGee a standing ovation for his last passionate speech on the spirit of Confederation.

Then McGee put on his overcoat, gloves, and new white top hat and left the newly built centre block of parliament. As he started his slow walk back to his boarding house a short distance away, a full moon beamed down on him.

"Good night, Mr. McGee," called John Buckley, a House of Commons employee, as McGee turned onto Sparks Street.

"Good morning," joked McGee. "It's morning now."

Those were his last words.

His landlady, Mrs. Trotter, heard the drumming of feet and what sounded like a firecracker outside her front door. When she went to investigate, she found a figure slumped against the blood-speckled doorway. It was her lodger, shot to death. The bullet had entered the back of his head, passed through his skull, and exited through his mouth. The gun had been fired at such close range that some of McGee's teeth were found embedded in the doorpost.

McGee was a close friend and drinking buddy of John A. Macdonald, also a Father of Confederation and now prime minister of Canada. Sir John A., as he was called, was devastated when wakened with the news that his companion had just been shot. He rushed at once to the scene of the murder and helped carry his dead friend into the house. He returned home, covered in blood and, as Macdonald's wife Agnes described him, "much agitated," with a face "ghostly white."

A massive manhunt was launched, with more than two hundred people arrested in the police sweep. That afternoon, Sir John A. delivered a sombre tribute in the House of Commons to the "foully murdered" McGee. Flags flew at half-mast in Ottawa, Montreal, and Toronto. The mayor of Ottawa posted a reward of $2,000 for information leading to the capture of the killer, and the federal government and provinces of Ontario and Quebec between them offered another $10,000.

The nation was in shock.

McGee, a short, chunky man with shaggy black hair, was nothing remarkable to look at. But he was an inspired public speaker with a magnetic personality. On the day he died, *The Globe* described him as "marvellously eloquent.... His wit — his power of sarcasm — his readiness in reply — his aptness in quotation — his pathos which melted to tears, and his broad humour which convulsed with laughter — were all undoubtedly of a very high order."

In the period leading up to Confederation, McGee had fired up audiences with his enthusiasm and his vision of a free, tolerant, and united Canada. As noted by Fennings Taylor in a 1868 sketch of McGee's life and death, McGee presented this ideal to fellow provincial parliamentarians

Thomas D'Arcy McGee, statesman, journalist, public speaker, and poet. This portrait is dated 1868, the year that McGee was felled by an assassin's bullet, becoming the only Canadian federal politician ever to be assassinated.

in 1860. "I see in the not remote distance," he said, "one great nationality, bound, like the shield of Achilles, by the blue rim of ocean. I see it quartered into many communities, each disposing of its internal affairs, but all bound together by free institutions.... I see within the round of that shield the peaks of the western mountains and the crests of the eastern waves."

McGee was a man of action as well as a visionary. Between 1864 and 1866, his key role in the negotiations with Britain that led to the founding of the Dominion of Canada prompted many to describe him as *the* (rather than *a*) Father of Confederation.

But McGee wasn't always a Canadian nationalist, loyal to the British Crown. Ironically, he started off as a fiery revolutionary. In Ireland, where he was born in Carlingford in 1825 and raised as a Roman Catholic, and in the United States, where he landed as a seventeen-year-old in 1842 to work as a newspaperman, he was strongly in favour of armed rebellion *against* British rule in Ireland. On his return to his native country in 1845, he became so politically active that the British issued a warrant for his arrest, and he had to flee back to the States, disguised as a priest.

McGee became increasingly disenchanted with what he regarded as the discrimination and exploitation experienced by Irish immigrants in the United States. And once he moved to Canada in 1857 on the invitation of a group of Irish Catholics to start up the *New Era* newspaper in Montreal, he expressed his opinions even more forcefully, declaring that minorities, including Catholics, were much better off in Canada than in the United States.

McGee was dirt poor in spite of his multiple professional activities as a charismatic politician, public speaker, journalist, and poet. Fortunately, he had powerful friends who were happy to help out. He owned a home on St. Catherine Street in Montreal, where he lived with his wife, Mary, and their two young daughters, Frasa and Peggy. The house, decorated with shamrocks, the symbol of Ireland, had been a gift from supporters.

But violence and danger stalked McGee throughout his life, and he made many enemies.

His sharp tongue and acid wit wounded his political opponents. Much more seriously, he became a harsh critic of an Irish separatist movement and secret society called the Fenian Brotherhood.

The Fenian Brotherhood was founded in the United States in 1858 with the aim of violently overthrowing British rule in Ireland. The Fenians had a large number of followers in the States, with fewer in Canada. In 1866, the U.S. branch, for the most part Irish-American veterans of the American Civil War, launched two raids — or invasions, depending on who you spoke to — into Canada. The first one into New Brunswick was a complete failure. The other incursion from Buffalo, New York, over the Niagara River and into Ontario was a great success; but the inexperience of the commanding officer led to the withdrawal of the Fenian forces.

McGee went on the offensive, fearing that Fenian activities would lead to a violent backlash against the Irish in Canada.

"Secret Societies are like what the farmers in Ireland used to say of scotch grass," he wrote in the *Montreal Gazette*. "The only way to destroy it is to cut it out by the roots and burn it into powder." He threatened to publish "documents which would put in their proper position the Fenians of Montreal."

And that, according to historian David A. Wilson in his biography of Thomas D'Arcy McGee, was when the death threats began. One anonymous letter writer warned that McGee would be assassinated if he revealed any information about the Fenians in Montreal. Another letter, wrapped up in a Fenian newspaper, contained a drawing of a gallows and a coffin.

So when McGee was assassinated, suspicion immediately fell on the Fenians. Within twenty-four hours, police arrested Patrick James Whelan, a twenty-eight-year-old Irish immigrant with strong Fenian associations. They found a fully loaded .32 calibre Smith & Wesson revolver in his coat pocket. He was charged with the murder of Thomas D'Arcy McGee.

Easter Monday, 1868: on what would have been his forty-third birthday, McGee was given a state funeral — Canada's first — in Montreal. The turnout was enormous, partly because the new Grand Trunk Railway, which had been strongly championed by McGee, offered cheap fares to attendees from all around the country. Some 80,000 people (the population of Montreal at that time was 105,000) silently lined the streets, many hanging out of windows or standing on the rooftops, as the procession passed by. The coffin was carried in a sixteen-foot-long, sixteen-foot-high funeral

Patrick James Whelan was an Irish immigrant associated with the Fenian Brotherhood, a secret society that aimed to violently overthrow British rule in Ireland. Whelan's execution for the assassination of Thomas D'Arcy McGee still stirs up controversy today.

carriage drawn by six grey horses with black ostrich plumes on their heads. Guns were fired every minute, and military bands along the way played George Frideric Handel's "Dead March." McGee was buried in his family mausoleum at the Notre-Dame-des-Neiges Cemetery in Montreal.

And what of Patrick Whelan?

His trial began in Ottawa in September 1868. Newspapers of the day called him "the tailor with the sandy whiskers." The *Ottawa Times* reported that "as point after point of evidence was brought out during his trial, his uncontrollable restlessness of body, his constant turning of the head, his knitted brows, his staring eyes and twitching mouth, gave evident marks of his anxiety." On the eighth (and last) day of his trial, he wore plain black. He probably knew what was coming. He was found guilty and sentenced to death by hanging.

Whelan swore that he was innocent. "I am here standing on the brink of my grave," he told the court, "and I wish to declare to you and to my God ... that I never committed this deed, and that, I know in my heart and soul."

His lawyers launched two appeals against his sentence: both failed. In the interim, he languished on death row at the Carleton County Gaol in Ottawa.

The year 1869 was known as the Year of the Big Snow in the Ottawa Valley. It began with a bone-chilling blizzard on February 11, and it

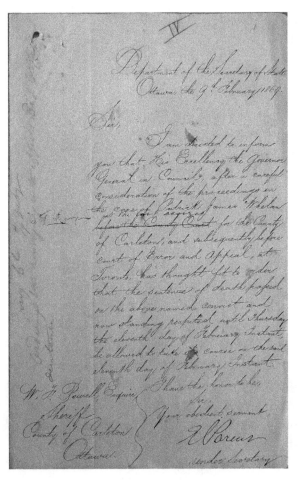

Letter dated February 9, 1869, from the Department of the Secretary of State in Ottawa to sheriff W.F. Powell of the County of Carleton, advising him that the execution of Patrick James Whelan should proceed as planned.

continued to snow without let-up until St. Patrick's Day on March 17. Impenetrable six-and-a-half-foot-high drifts covered fields and villages, roads disappeared, farms and communities were totally isolated, and cattle perished in their stalls.

Patrick Whelan was hanged at the Carleton County Gaol in Ottawa on the first morning of the snowstorm. In spite of the evil weather, more than five thousand people showed up for his execution. He went to his death with the words "God save Ireland! And God save my soul!" on his lips. It took seven long minutes for Whelan to die.

Executed individuals were usually buried in the cemetery of the prison where their hanging took place. Whelan was no exception: he was interred in an unmarked grave in the courtyard of the jail. But in 2002, following petitions from his family, a box of earth was dug up from the jail yard and taken to Montreal to be symbolically reburied beside Whelan's widow's remains in the Notre-Dame-Des-Neiges Cemetery.

How ironic that memorials to the two men — one murdered, the other hanged for his murder — now stand in such close proximity.

But was Whelan actually guilty of the crime?

Many say yes. Whelan, like McGee, lived in Montreal. As noted by Wilson, Whelan was either a Fenian or a Fenian sympathizer, and he hated McGee. He had been stalking McGee for months, following him to Ottawa when McGee went there on parliamentary business. He was in the visitors' gallery at the House of Commons on the morning of the murder. He left the House at the same time as McGee and had no alibi for the time between 2:10 and 2:30 a.m. When the police arrested him, they found his Smith & Wesson revolver, which looked as though it had recently been fired. During Whelan's trial, Joseph Faulkner, a tailor who worked with him in Montreal, testified that Whelan had said that McGee "was a traitor and deserved to be shot." Another witness from Montreal, Alexander J. Turner, told the court that after McGee was elected to parliament, Whelan had threatened to "blow his bloody brains out before the session is over."

On the other hand, there were signs that justice had not been done. Sir John A., McGee's great friend, sat next to Judge William Buell Richards during the trial, which could have seriously influenced the jury's decisions. Turner, whose evidence was particularly damaging to Whelan, was accused by the defence of lying in the hope of claiming a chunk of the reward money. In the two failed appeals against Whelan's death sentence, Judge Richards, by now promoted to his new role as chief justice of Ontario, cast a deciding vote instead of stepping aside to make sure the process would be unbiased.

Other troubling questions remain. Witnesses had described a mysterious man sitting next to Whelan in the House of Commons on the night of the murder, making threatening gestures as McGee gave his final speech. Who was this suspect, and why was nothing done to investigate him further? What about reports of a horse and buggy seen speeding away from the crime scene? Was Whelan telling the truth when he said, just before he was hanged, "I know the man who shot Mr. McGee," but that he was not prepared to rat on him? Could it be, as Wilson suggests, that Whelan was not a lone assassin but part of a hit squad?

And what about the murder weapon? Some commentators say that the evidence linking Whelan's revolver to the crime was weak and circumstantial. This argument was tested when the gun turned up in 1973 in the possession of a private owner, Scott Renwick, an auto mechanic from Dundalk, Ontario. It seems that the original investigating officer had kept the firearm, which was a perfectly acceptable practice in the 1800s, and it was passed down through his family from generation to generation.

With new forensic tools available, Ontario's Centre of Forensic Sciences found that a bullet fired from the gun looked a lot like the McGee bullet. This did not prove conclusively that Whelan shot McGee, but it did show that McGee was shot with the same kind of gun and ammunition Whelan was carrying when he was arrested.

Whether Whelan was guilty or not, this case has gone down in the record books. Thomas D'Arcy McGee is the only Canadian federal politician, and a very high-profile one at that, ever to be assassinated.

Patrick Whelan was the second-last individual in Canada to be officially executed in a public space. Later in 1869, the year Whelan was hanged, Sir John A. Macdonald signed a bill in an attempt to ensure that, beginning the following year, hangings would take place either out of the public's view or with restrictions on the number of onlookers allowed to attend.

CHAPTER 4

Crowd Control

How would you feel if you went to all the trouble of organizing a hanging and no one came? If you were John Macdonald, sheriff of Huron County, Ontario, on December 7, 1869, you would be exceptionally relieved. Macdonald surreptitiously changed the time of the hanging at the Huron County Gaol in Goderich to 8:45 a.m., hours earlier than scheduled, to keep the crowds away. Imagine his shock when, in spite of the early start, around three hundred people still showed up. The execution was mercifully quick and efficient, as noted by John Melady in his book *Double Trap*, and after thirty minutes the corpse was cut down, placed in a pine coffin, and taken to the train station. On the way, it passed thousands of people heading in the opposite direction, all hell-bent on watching the spectacle unfold later that morning.

The fact is, Sheriff Macdonald had every reason to be afraid, very afraid. The hangman was clearly nervous, too. He had blackened his face and hands to disguise himself, leading the *Huron Expositor* to describe him as "fiendish looking." The case had ignited a fiery reaction in the community. Many felt that the prisoner, the only person convicted for the crime, had been betrayed by his associates and entrapped by a police informant. In addition, out-of-control mobs at public executions were a fearsome reality. Both the sheriff and the executioner might well have read, or heard, of the shenanigans at the execution of Edgar Harter exactly nine years previously in not-too-distant Brockville, Ontario. As the *Brockville Monitor* reported:

> Wet and exceedingly unpleasant as the day was, it did not prevent crowds of morbid sightseers thronging from all quarters into Brockville to see the execution … until at length some four thousand strangers swarmed along the streets.… Hard-looking men, and brazen-looking women, and blackguard boys might be encountered at every point. As the necessary sequence of such an assemblage there were laughing and shouting, and snowballing, and ribaldry prevailing, with some fighting and drunkenness, leading one to question very seriously the propriety of public executions, which usually draw such indecent mobs together.

Fortunately for Sheriff Macdonald and his henchman, the disappointment of the hordes when they realized they had been duped did not explode into violence as it could so easily have done.

It must be said, though, that when it came to crowd misbehaviour, Canada couldn't hope to compete with the Brits. A case in point was the execution of husband-and-wife murderers Frederick and Marie Manning outside Horsemonger Lane Gaol in London, England, in 1849. According to a horrified Charles Dickens in a letter to *The Times*, "thieves, low prostitutes, ruffians and vagabonds of every kind, flocked on to the ground, with every variety of offensive and foul behaviour. Fightings, faintings, whistlings, imitations of Punch, brutal jokes, tumultuous demonstrations of indecent delight when swooning women were dragged out of the crowd by the police with their dresses disordered, gave a new zest to the general entertainment."

The man hanged at the Huron County Gaol in Goderich that harsh December morning in 1869 was Nicholas Melady Jr., convicted of brutally murdering his father, Nicholas Sr., also known as Old Melady, on June 6, 1868. Also murdered that day was Melady Jr.'s pregnant stepmother, Ellen. The *Huron Signal* described a neighbour's visit to the Melady farmhouse just outside Seaforth the following morning, where "a most shocking sight met his horrified gaze. At the bedroom door lay Mr. Mellady [*sic*] shot through the head, and at the bedside was stretched the lifeless corpse of his wife, her skull split open and her body otherwise horribly mutilated.... The walls and floors of the rooms were literally covered with the gore of the victims."

The case was dreadful in the extreme. Old Melady was a wealthy farmer generally reviled in the area for his hard drinking and foul temper. He was particularly hated by his six children, especially since he frequently threatened to disinherit them, promising to leave his fortune to his second wife and their unborn baby. The whole family seemed to have been involved in a conspiracy to kill the old man, but Nicholas Jr. went to the gallows alone.

"*Cherchez la femme,*" the old saying goes, and there certainly was a woman in this case: Jenny Smith (real name Janet Cooke), a beautiful, young police informer planted in the prison where Melady Jr. was being held. In cahoots with veteran police detective William Smith, Jenny posed as a prisoner with the aim of insinuating herself into Melady's affections and possibly wresting a confession from him. She communicated with Melady through his cell window, which overlooked the women's exercise yard. He fell in love with her and was shattered when she gave evidence against him at his trial. He was found "guilty as charged" and sentenced to death.

As described by author John Melady (yes, he is family — he claims Nicholas Jr. as his cousin), the scaffold was built atop the east wall of the jail, with the stairs inside the wall and the trap on the outside. So Melady dropped to his death on the same side of the wall as the curious onlookers gathered below.

That made it, technically, the last hanging in a public place in Canada. In 1869, *An Act respecting Procedure in Criminal Cases, and other matters relating to Criminal Law, 1869,* introduced some important changes. Section 109 of this piece of legislation, which was based almost word for word on a similar British law passed in 1868, provided that "judgment of death to be executed on any prisoner after the coming into force of this Act, shall be carried into effect within the walls of the prison in which the offender is confined at the time of execution." Additionally, at

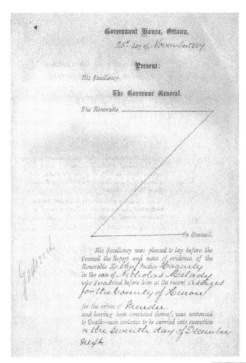

An Order-in-Council was issued on November 25, 1869, refusing a request to commute Nicholas Melady's death sentence. Melady's hanging on December 7 was the last one in a public place in Canada.

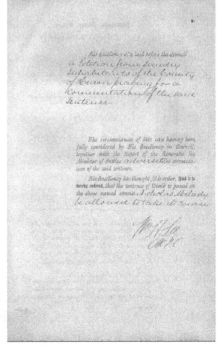

the beginning of 1870, an Order-in-Council containing a series of rules and regulations written by Prime Minister John A. Macdonald, in his capacity as minister of justice, attempted to impose uniformity in how executions were carried out across Canada.

So public executions went private, hidden behind prison walls. The official act reflected the extreme discomfort felt by polite nineteenth-century Victorian society in the face of the violence, obscenity, callousness, and contempt shown by mobs at a hanging. But an uneasy tension remained: if you prevented the public from attending hangings because they behaved so badly, how could you make sure that executions would remain a powerful deterrent and that their retributive message — if you commit a crime, you will be punished — would endure in the public consciousness?

As Ken Leyton-Brown observes: "Means had to be found to enable the continuation of public involvement, in what was to be considered private execution." The authorities tried to deal with this thorny problem by allowing representatives of the public to be present at executions — the sheriff who was handling the execution, the gaoler, doctors or surgeons, justices of the peace, prisoners' relatives "or other persons as it seems to the Sheriff proper to admit within the prison for the purpose," and, of course, ministers of religion. Also, the 1869 act provided for certain procedures to be followed after an execution: a doctor was to examine the body of the hanged person and sign a death certificate; the sheriff was to sign a declaration that the person had been executed; and a coroner's inquest was to be held.

Other measures to advertise that an execution was taking place were specified in the rules and regulations. Rule 3, for example, provided for "a black flag to be hoisted at the moment of execution, upon a staff placed upon an elevated and conspicuous part of the prison, and to remain displayed for one hour." So, on December 13, 1901, after Joseph Ernest Laplaine was executed in Montreal, Quebec, for the murder of his landlady Valérie Charbonneau, the *Montreal Gazette* reported that "with the carrying out of the law's decree the black flag was hoisted on the jail, proclaiming to the six hundred or so persons who had gathered outside that Laplaine had paid the penalty of his crime."

According to Rule 4 of the rules and regs, the bell of the prison or of a neighbouring church was to be "tolled for fifteen minutes before, and fifteen minutes after the execution." As a variant of this requirement, when Wilbert Coffin was hanged at Montreal's infamous Bordeaux jail on February 10, 1956, a black flag flew and a bell rang out seven solemn times to announce his death.

So now that executions had moved inside prison walls, you might assume that the days of the inappropriate carnival-like antics of huge crowds at a hanging would be over.

You would be wrong.

Remember that the sheriff was allowed by the *Procedure in Criminal Cases* act to invite members of the public to attend hangings if he thought it appropriate to do so? Well, he often did. It was not uncommon for as many as two hundred people, among them newspaper reporters, to be given permits to witness a hanging. Sometimes these permissions were used to ram home a message. In 1885, a group of Indigenous men, the so-called "Cree Eight," were tried for murder and sentenced to hang for their involvement in the North-West Rebellion, the same uprising that saw Louis Riel go to the gallows. The men were hanged together in Battleford, Saskatchewan, on a twenty-foot-high scaffold specially built for the purpose. As a chilling reminder of the power and authority of the state, hundreds of local Indigenous people were rounded up to watch the execution, among them all the students of the Battleford Industrial School.

Gatecrashing was common. Witness the scene when Joseph N. Thibeau of Annapolis County, Nova Scotia, was hanged in February 1881. Thibeau had been convicted for the murder by fire of Charlotte Hill, a resident of the poorhouse that he ran. The *New York Times* described the "wild disorder" of a horde of around a thousand spectators, among them women and children:

> Toward daylight teams of every description began to pour into the town, and soon after 6 o'clock the crowd began to gather in front of the jail inclosure [*sic*]. Several crowds, principally from the country, were inflamed with liquor.... With shouts and yells, the mob rushed

toward the fence. Clergymen, constables, and citizens tried in every way to restrain the throng, but all to no purpose. Huge beams were used as battering rams, and once an opening was made, poles and hands were used, and the whole front of the high, strong fence was in a few minutes torn down. The scene was one of the most disgraceful ever seen.

Even if you did manage to keep the public out, it was not always easy to shield the gallows from view. Spectators would clamber onto walls and rooftops to watch a hanging. Take the sensational case of Thomas Nulty, age twenty-one, of Rawdon, Quebec, who butchered his four younger siblings with an axe. There were grave doubts as to whether he was responsible for his actions, but the jury found him guilty with no recommendation for mercy. He was hanged in May 1898 at the Joliette Gaol, Quebec. According to the *Ottawa Journal*, Nulty died "stolid and apparently unconcerned." By contrast, "fully a thousand laughing, jeering men were present.... So badly had matters been arranged that anyone who possessed a ladder sufficiently long, made up a party of himself and friends, selected a nice sunny spot on either the roof of the gaol or the gaol shed, and stayed there.... The whole thing seemed like a circus, so much so that even Radcliffe, the executioner, lodged a formal complaint."

It was especially difficult to ensure privacy in smaller centres. As quoted in Terry Boyle's *Fit to Be Tied*, Blanche Grant, a young girl living in Parry Sound, Ontario, described the hanging of train robber John Burowski in December 1928 for the murder of Thomas Jackson, a farmer from Waubamik. She wrote that the top beam of the scaffold was clearly visible above the Parry Sound Gaol wall. To mask this, "the wall height was increased by a solid paper fence on the day of the execution.... At midnight of that crucial day the courtyard was ablaze with lights and the shadows of the action could be seen on the paper fence."

On occasion, it did seem as though the situation actually *was* improving. Unlike the chaotic scenes at Thibeau's and Nulty's executions, all was calm and orderly when Raoul Brodeur was hanged in Sweetsburg, Quebec, in December 1923. Hangman Arthur Ellis sprang the trap, the black flag was hoisted, and the bells of the town church tolled. The jail doctor examined the body and pronounced Brodeur dead. The body was cut down, and an inquest was held immediately. As the *Granby Leader-Mail* commented, "many persons attempted to witness the hanging, but only the officials and newspapermen were allowed in the jail courtyard."

Things seemed so well organized that in 1928, after an incident in the United States where a newsman smuggled a camera into the death chamber at the notorious Sing Sing prison near New York City, the *Southeast Missourian* heaped praise on Canada. At a recent hanging in Canada, "not even a porter was permitted to see the hanging.… The raising of the black flag was all that was made public about the execution itself.… The Canadian method of executing criminals, so far as publicity is concerned, is better than ours."

Then an incident in March 1935 brought the horrors of hanging squarely to the forefront again. "A Ghastly Hanging" trumpeted the *Ottawa Citizen* in 1935, when Tommasina Teolis was decapitated during her execution at the Bordeaux jail in Montreal. Enough of capital punishment. This "ghastly and barbarous episode should be made impossible in the future," was the newspaper's bitter lament. But hangings continued. All that ended in 1935, as a result of this event, was the practice of giving out tickets to the public to watch them.

One step forward, two steps back. Take the execution of Peter Balcombe in Cornwall, Ontario. In this high-profile case, Balcombe, a young married Canadian army lieutenant, was arrested and charged with murder after the nude body of Marie-Anne Carrier, a women's reserve army sergeant, was found stabbed to death in a ditch near Iroquois, Ontario. Balcombe had promised to leave his wife for Marie-Anne, but chose a more chilling way of extricating himself from a tricky relationship.

According to the *Toronto Star*, when Balcombe met his end, "the canvas-covered top of the gallows was plainly visible from the street. The crowd, many of them teenagers, including many young girls, was in a holiday mood, shooting off firecrackers, joking and laughing for more than two hours before the execution took place. Several times, police details had to clear the streets so vehicles could pass as the onlookers pressed forward for better vantage points."

This happened in 1954: eighty-five years after executions were supposedly removed from public spaces and just eight years before the very last executions in Canada. Nothing, it seemed, could effectively slam the door shut on the frenzied crowds who turned out in droves, clambered onto rooftops, or stormed prison gates to witness an execution.

CHAPTER 5

The Hangman's Job

According to the law, the federal government played no role in organizing executions in Canada. As the *Montreal Gazette* put it in 1936: "The sheriff of a judicial district is the man charged with the execution of the laws, civil or criminal, and consequently is engaged in either hanging people or seizing their furniture, or otherwise annoying them."

The requirement to organize hangings made the local sheriffs feel *really* uncomfortable. It could even make them sick. Beneath the headline "Sheriff Cannot Find a Hangman," *The Globe* reported in March 1912 that E. Martin, sheriff of Fraserville, Quebec, was "seriously ill from worry over his inability to hire a hangman. With an execution only eight days off, he cannot locate anyone willing and able to take the position, and may have to undertake the task himself."

And sheriffs did not relish the idea of conducting hangings themselves, especially because the condemned person was very likely to be someone they knew. They were also not confident of their expertise to carry out the job without bungling it.

There were individuals prepared to step in, though. *The Globe* published a letter in July 1910 that read in part: "I wish to ask you if there is any possible chance for securing the position of assistant executioner.... I am willing to carry out anything that the law requires in connection with the position. I am an Englishman, 34 years old, strong and possessing all kinds of nerve, all of which are absolutely necessary for the position."

So what would be the basic qualifications for anyone wanting to apply?

The Globe letter writer fulfilled the very first requirement, which was that you had to be a man. No hangwomen or hangpersons were allowed.

You would also have to be prepared to travel — a lot. Executions generally took place at a jail near where the crime had been committed and where the trial was held, and the hangman had to make his way there. So you could find yourself taking long, boring train journeys to dots on the map like Lytton, British Columbia, or L'Orignal, Ontario, or Battleford, Saskatchewan, or Dorchester, New Brunswick. And you might end up paying for your own rail tickets.

Carrying your own tools with you — a black hood and leather straps to bind the arms and legs of the prisoner, for example — was essential. You might even have to buy and prepare the rope used for the hanging. New rope is very elastic, and you would need to stretch it out by suspending a heavy weight from it for a few days before the hanging. If you were travelling to those dots on the map — like Lytton or L'Orignal or Battleford or Dorchester — you might have to rely on a hastily and perhaps shoddily built scaffold provided on site, or bring along your own. As noted by Ken Leyton-Brown, this was the preferred solution of one of Canada's best-known and busiest hangmen, Arthur Ellis. His portable kit was painted an eye-popping shade of red.

To be avoided at all costs was the kind of situation that occurred in December 1879, when a Cree hunter and trapper named Ka-Ki-Si-Kutchin or Swift Runner was hanged at Fort Saskatchewan Gaol, Alberta, for the murder of eight members of his family. According to the *Edmonton Journal*, crisis followed crisis on the day of the execution: the sheriff was delayed by brutally cold weather; the inexperienced hangman forgot to bring straps for pinioning the condemned man's arms and legs; and, unaccustomed as they were to public hangings, the crowd of onlookers burned the wooden trap from the gallows to provide some heat. As officials scurried around to get the scaffold ready again, the prisoner cheerfully offered to kill himself with a tomahawk and save the hangman further trouble.

Another important requirement for a hangman was a solid understanding of the mathematics of hanging. You would have to calculate the drop or length of rope used for each hanging depending on the weight of the condemned person. If all went according to plan, the fall would dislocate the vertebrae when the trap was sprung, causing a quick death. This was not an exact science, however, and mistakes did happen. It took seven minutes for Patrick Whelan to die, remember? The drop was probably too short. And in Rimouski, Quebec, in 1882, the hanging of murderer François Moreau was badly bungled. Although his death was instantaneous, the drop was far too long, and his head, according to the *Toronto Daily Mail*, was nearly separated from his body.

You would also have to deal with the often extreme hostility of the community. The locals were very unhappy when someone from the district went to the gallows, and they often took out their anger on the hangman. Look at what happened in 1872 after the hanging of Vildebon Bissonnette at the Montmagny Gaol, Quebec, for example. As they were leaving town by train, the two hangmen, a French Canadian and a Scot, started discussing the part they had played in the execution. Their fellow passengers went wild and beat both of them up. So, while on the job, you might want to disguise yourself with a mask and a false moustache, and you should be prepared to leave town in a hurry.

As a hangman, you would certainly have to cope with unruly or uncooperative prisoners. In 1899, Benjamin Parrott, a carter from Hamilton, Ontario, was hanged for the brutal assault and murder of his mother. The *Daily Mail and Empire* reported that he was possibly insane and had attacked his family before, but that he was generally all right except when he had been drinking. He was clearly under the influence of the demon drink when he felled his mother with three axe blows to the head after a family altercation. On the day he was executed, Parrott asked for and was given some brandy just before leaving his cell, and he cursed the hangman all the way to the scaffold. In 1911, Francesco Grevola, convicted of the murder of a fellow Italian in Montreal, suffered a complete collapse and had to be half dragged, half carried to the gallows. A more active resistance was offered by Lawrence Vincent, a carnival worker hanged in 1955 at the Oakalla Prison in Burnaby, British Columbia, for strangling a young girl to death. He fought off hangman Camille Branchaud when the latter entered his cell to pinion his arms and followed up by physically attacking and yelling insults at Branchaud on the scaffold.

As for the bottom line — well, the pay could vary. Unfortunately, like most of the hangmen, you probably wouldn't get a regular salary. As reported in *The Globe* in December 1912, hangman Arthur Ellis complained: "I don't know how I drifted into the business, but I am tired of it and will quit unless I can get a living out of it." At that time, sheriffs in larger cities were paying him $75 per hanging, and in smaller centres the pay was $50. As ropes were never reused, cash-strapped executioners sometimes considered supplementing their income by cutting them up and selling the lengths as souvenirs.

With all these complicated requirements, sheriffs started to rely heavily on a small group of professionals who were sufficiently skilled to do the job quickly and efficiently. These men were sometimes called "Canada's Executioners." One of the first of these experts after Confederation was a man named John Robert Radclive.

Growing up in Britain, John Radclive did not plan to be a hangman — he wanted to be a clergyman. "But I was no hypocrite and I gave it up." In a 2007 article in the *Toronto Star*, Patrick Cain noted that Radclive joined the Royal Navy instead, where his duties included hanging pirates in the South China Sea. He also spent some years in the British army, fighting in India.

After his arrival in Canada in 1887, Radclive went into a new line of work. But his salary as a steward at Toronto's trendy Sunnyside Boating Club wasn't enough to support his wife and four children. Fortunately, he had a useful skill to fall back on — after leaving the army, he had trained with William Marwood, Britain's official executioner. So Radclive started working part-time as a hangman. Some members of the boating club merely laughed when the news trickled out that their steward was moonlighting as a hangman. But an influential member who was an inspector with the North-West Mounted Police complained to the club owners about having his drinks served by a "common hangman." Radclive refused to keep his extracurricular activities a secret, and he was fired for "lack of discretion."

So again, Radclive found himself changing careers: in 1892, he became Canada's first professional hangman. He hanged at least sixty-nine people, although the number could be as high as one hundred and fifty — in those days, record keeping was not very accurate.

In the early years, Cain writes, Radclive did quite well financially — he seems to have been the only hangman to be paid a regular retainer of $750 a year, plus an additional fee and expenses for every hanging he performed. In 1893, he bought a house on Sorauren Avenue in Parkdale, Toronto, and he later lived on Fern Avenue in the same area. Over time he seems to have been tolerated in the neighbourhood in spite of his grisly profession. According to a neighbour, "The little children who weren't frightened of him just loved him."

But Radclive enjoyed his sinister reputation as a hangman, and his often offensive behaviour ensured that not everybody loved him.

In 1890, a high-profile murder case kept the public glued to their newspapers. This was the so-called "Blenheim Swamp Murder." John Reginald Birchall, a charming British con man masquerading as a member of the English aristocracy, lured a prospective business part-ner, also an Englishman, to a remote and swampy area near Woodstock, Ontario. There he shot him twice in the back of the head. Through a series of coincidences and some brilliant investigative work by John "Old Never-Let-Go" Murray, chief detective for the province of Ontario, Birchall was arrested and tried for murder. After an eight-day trial, he was found guilty and sentenced to be hanged on November 14, 1890, with John Radclive officiating.

The day after the execution, the *Toronto World*, in a report stretch-ing over four whole columns, recreated the drama of Birchall's last night on earth. Tucked in among reams of information on the poignant last meeting between Birchall and his wife, the relationship of Birchall with his spiritual advisor, and Birchall's personal preparations before the hanging was this unflattering snippet: "Meantime, in the corridor below, the hangman was peacefully reclining on a lounge, with the sound sleep of a babe but the snore of a traction engine.... The executioner was in an unusually cheerful mood, and during wakeful moments joked with the turnkey, the pencil pushers [newspaper reporters] and others." The

Huron Expositor was even more withering: "The hangman disgusted everyone by his noisy talking in the jail during the night."

Twelve years later, Radclive also infuriated the people of Hull, Quebec, the day before the execution of Stanislaus Lacroix in March 1902.

Lacroix was a violently jealous man. He had pumped three bullets into his estranged wife, killing her, and he also murdered an elderly neighbour he suspected, wrongly, of having a relationship with her. During his trial, he gave the court the names of numerous other people on his hit list, including the parish priest. So Lacroix was not exactly the perfect citizen. However, when Radclive got drunk in the pub and boasted loudly that he was in town to hang Lacroix, the locals exploded with rage. They attacked Radclive; it took a wagonload of policemen to rescue him. For his own protection, he spent the night in the same jail as the man he was to hang the next day. The *Ottawa Citizen* reported that at the execution Radclive's eyes "were black and badly swollen and his face was adorned with court plaster, giving evidence of the rough treatment he received yesterday."

By that time, Radclive was drinking so heavily that even seasoned reporters and prison officials were shocked. In 1910, a reporter from the *Telegram* sat with him in a Stratford, Ontario, hotel room on a Sunday afternoon, the day before a hanging, and watched him drink beer after beer "from the bottle, never using a glass."

It is said that Radclive started drinking excessively after the double hanging of a man and a woman in 1899. Samuel Parslow and Cordélia Viau were tried separately and both convicted of murdering Viau's husband in Ste-Scholastique, Quebec. Before the execution, what a Montreal newspaper called a "howling mob" of two thousand swarmed the prison and tried to batter down the gate. The provincial police had to fire their revolvers in the air to break up the crowd. After the hanging, some of the six hundred spectators permitted to witness the execution from inside the prison yard charged the scaffold and ripped off the black cloth that shielded the bodies from public view. The behaviour of the frenzied crowd had unnerved Radclive so much that he drank an entire bottle of brandy that night.

While he was initially cool and controlled at a hanging, the fear of bungling started preying on Radclive's mind. As noted by Pfeifer and

Leyton-Brown in *Death by Rope*, after something went wrong in 1902 at the execution of Walter Gordon in Brandon, Manitoba, Radclive, shaking like a leaf, exclaimed to the sheriff: "My God, it's terrible, it's terrible. Why did I ever start at this business?"

Radclive retired in 1910 — his last hanging was in July of that year. In February 1911, he died in Toronto of cirrhosis, a liver disease no doubt caused by his excessive drinking. He was fifty-five years old and penniless. His wife had left him and gone back to Britain with two of their children, and he had lost contact with the two who remained in Canada. They were ashamed of their father's profession.

As quoted by Kenneth Saunders in *The Rectory Murder: The Mysterious Crime that Shocked Turn-of-the-Century New Brunswick*, Radclive described his nightmarish visions in an interview shortly before his death: "Now at night when I lie down, I start up with a roar as victim after victim comes up before me. I can see them on the trap, waiting a second before they meet their Maker. They haunt me and taunt me until I am nearly crazy with an unearthly fear."

John Robert Radclive died alone, despised for his job, rejected by his family, and haunted by his inner demons.

The famous English author George Orwell once wrote: "Most people approve of capital punishment, but most people wouldn't do the hangman's job."

Would *you*?

CHAPTER 6

Treason:
The Case Against Louis Riel

Louis Riel did not sleep as the clock ticked away his last few hours on earth. He spent most of the night on his knees, praying. At 11:00 p.m., he ate a small meal of bread, milk, and three raw eggs. At 7:00 a.m. the following morning, November 16, 1885, Catholic priests Father André and Father McWilliams administered the last rites to prepare the doomed man for death. Riel looked pale but calm. Wearing a short black coat, a woollen shirt and collar, dark grey tweed pants, and moccasins, he started the slow walk to the scaffold from his cell at the North-West Mounted Police barracks in Regina, Saskatchewan. The Mounties had thrown a cordon around the scaffold, which had been set up in a fenced enclosure adjacent to the loft. The only access was through a window. Riel and his spiritual advisors knelt and prayed at the opening, then they stepped outside.

At 8:15, on a signal from the deputy sheriff, the hangman, Jack Henderson, came forward with straps to pinion Riel's arms for the hanging.

"Louis Riel," he reportedly whispered, "do you know me? You had me once and I got away from you. I have you now and you'll not get away from me!"

Did Louis Riel hear those vicious words? Was he completely lost in prayer, or did his mind flash back through the years in a final attempt to make sense of what had brought him to that place?

Louis Riel was the eldest of eleven children born to Louis Riel and Julie Lagimonière at the Red River Settlement in what is now Manitoba on October 22, 1844. He was one of six thousand French-speaking Catholic Métis (an Indigenous people with mixed white and First Nations ancestry). In his early teens, he was sent to school in Montreal; his vocation was to be a Catholic priest. But when his father died, he dropped out of religious studies and worked at a law firm in Montreal to support his family.

Riel was catapulted into political life before he reached twenty-five. At that time, Rupert's Land, which included what later became the three provinces of Manitoba, Alberta, and Saskatchewan, belonged to the Hudson's Bay Company. In 1868, the government of Canada started negotiations with the company to buy this huge expanse of territory. Eager to grab land on the prairies and not overly concerned about the people already living there, many English-speaking Ontarians started to push westward. Among them were members of the Orange Order, a Protestant social and political organization that was antagonistic toward French Canadians and Catholics.

The Métis of the Red River Settlement in Rupert's Land were afraid that they would lose their rights and traditional way of life when the sale went through. But who could help them hammer out an agreement with Canada? Louis Riel — energetic, educated, and bilingual — seemed like just the man for the job. He agreed to become their leader.

As noted by author and historian Lewis H. Thomas, Riel found a changed society on his return from the east. The population of the small, isolated settlement had swelled to nearly twelve thousand, most of them English-speaking Protestants hostile to the culture and values of the Métis. Like his people, Riel was concerned. He said the new settlers had come "to chase us from our homeland."

Riel acted promptly and forcefully, launching what was called the Red River Rebellion in 1869. He formed a provisional government for talks with the Canadian government, and his force of four hundred Métis took control of Upper Fort Garry (today's Winnipeg) without meeting resistance.

The prime minister of Canada, Sir John A. Macdonald, would probably have loved to dispatch troops to put down those pesky rebels. But with the national railroad still a distant dream, there was no way to send soldiers hurtling across the Canadian vastness in the depths of winter. Instead, Sir John A. negotiated with the Métis, and the province of Manitoba was created in 1870. The government of Canada guaranteed that land would not be taken from the Métis and that the French language would be recognized for the people of the prairies.

This was a stunning victory for Riel and his followers. But they made a fatal error, one that would come back to haunt Riel for the rest of his life and ultimately factor into his death.

During the rebellion, the Métis seized a number of prisoners. Among them was an aggressive Ontarian Orangeman named Thomas Scott, who took every possible opportunity to insult and disobey his guards. The Métis' patience finally snapped, and they demanded that he be punished. A military tribunal tried and convicted Scott for defying the authority of the provincial government. He was to be executed by firing squad.

Riel could have prevented the execution, but didn't. Whatever his motives (vengeance? fear of losing the support of his followers? the need to show Canada that the Métis should be taken seriously?), even the newspapers of the period were highly critical of what they saw as a disastrous misstep. The *Irish Canadian* commented that Riel's "first great mistake was the killing of Scott. That Scott brought his fate upon himself by foolhardy boasts and threats is generally conceded … but the act was nevertheless a criminal blunder of the first magnitude." And when Riel himself was executed in 1885, the *Quebec Daily Telegraph* made reference to "the shooting of Scott, for which Riel was beyond question more hounded to death in reality than for the last [Northwest] rebellion."

Riel's future executioner, Jack Henderson, was one of the men imprisoned with Scott during the rebellion. He swore to avenge both his own treatment and the death of his friend, now a martyr to the Orange cause.

Accused of Scott's murder in Protestant Canada, and with a reward of $5,000 offered for his capture, Riel became a wanted man. He fled to the United States, although he did return to Canada several times over the next few difficult years. He was even elected to the House of Commons for the Manitoba riding of Provencher, although he never actually took his seat in parliament. The stress finally took its toll, and Riel suffered

Louis Riel in 1875. The Métis leader from Manitoba, who launched two rebellions against the Canadian government in the late 1800s, was executed for high treason in 1885.

a mental breakdown. He spent two years in psychiatric hospitals in Quebec. From 1877 to 1884, he again lived in the United States, in both Keeseville, New York (close to Montreal), and Montana. He became an American citizen in 1883.

Riel returned to Canada for the last time in 1884. The Métis and First Nations people of Saskatchewan needed help to negotiate with the Canadian government for land rights and political power. At that time, Saskatchewan was part of the Northwest Territories, administered by the government of Canada; it became a province in 1905. The Métis called on Riel to work the same magic as he had in Manitoba in 1870. Although he responded to their call, Louis Riel was no longer the same man. He was fragile, both mentally and emotionally. He increasingly saw himself as the "Prophet of the Prairies," sent by God to lead his people.

Settlers in Saskatchewan, including whites and Métis, had a long list of objections regarding land claims and the collapse of land values in the area. Initially, they tried to petition Ottawa to redress these grievances. But when the government refused to act, merely saying that they would look into the problem, the protests were ramped up. In early 1885, Riel set up a provisional Métis government in Batoche on the South Saskatchewan River. In the spring of that year, the Métis launched an armed uprising called the Northwest Rebellion. It lasted just two months.

This time, advanced technology helped the Canadian government forces to win the day. They were able to speed across the country on the newly opened Canadian Pacific Railway, and at the decisive Battle of Batoche in Saskatchewan, which lasted four days, the army's superior manpower (eight hundred men against the rebels' two hundred) and firepower turned the tide. Their secret weapon was the American Gatling gun: operated by a single gunner, the Gatling spat out a hail of bullets, and the Métis fighters' rifles could offer little in response. The Canadians overran the rebels, and on May 12, 1885, the Northwest Rebellion was over. The rebels' military leader, Gabriel Dumont, escaped to the United States, and Riel, described as "cold and forlorn," surrendered to the North-West Mounted Police a few days later.

Riel was accused of high treason under a 1351 British act called the *Treason Act* — an offence punishable with death. Selecting a *British* statute dating back five hundred years was clearly a political decision, made by a government looking for a law that carried a mandatory death sentence. For that purpose, our own made-in-Canada laws were not good enough.

As a general rule in Canada, criminal trials were always held close to where the crime took place. Historically, there were solid reasons for this decision: it was easier to gather evidence locally; the judge and jury could visit the crime scene if necessary; and witnesses would not have to travel long distances to testify in court. Following this tradition, Riel should have been tried in or near Batoche. Instead, he was taken to Winnipeg for trial. This might have made some sense, as, in spite of his wanderings, Winnipeg was the place Riel called home. But, according to Thomas, when the authorities found out that, under Manitoba law, half the jury could be French speaking, he was quietly transferred to far-off Regina. There, he faced an all-white, English-speaking Protestant jury of six men.

Riel flatly refused to plead insanity, as advised by his lawyers. He understood that if he were declared insane, it would delegitimize his people's grievances against the Canadian government. His view was that he and his people had acted in self-defence. "I have a mission," he said. "I cannot fulfill my mission as long as I am looked upon as an insane being." As the trial progressed, relations between Riel and his lawyers broke down completely, and they asked the judge to deny Riel permission to speak.

When Riel did eventually have the opportunity to express his opinions in his final trial statement, he spoke so lucidly and rationally that he convinced the jury he was indeed sane. Ironically, this sealed his fate.

After the two-week trial, it took the jury less than an hour to come to a decision. The foreman, Francis Cosgrove, was reportedly "crying like a baby" when he announced the guilty verdict, with a recommendation for mercy. Judge Hugh Richardson, however, was not feeling particularly merciful that day. Finding Riel guilty of high treason, "a crime the most pernicious and greatest that man can commit," the judge sentenced him to death by hanging.

Decades later, one of the jurors, Edwin Brooks, said in a newspaper interview: "We tried Louis Riel for treason, but he was hanged for the murder of Thomas Scott."

Riel's lawyers appealed his sentence to the Court of Queen's Bench in Manitoba, but the court confirmed his conviction. The Judicial Committee of the Privy Council in London denied leave to further appeals. In spite of the fact that he was a U.S. citizen, the Americans declined to interfere, saying that "every country has the right to determine for itself what constitutes treason."

In a bizarre twist, Riel's secretary, William Henry Jackson, was captured after the Northwest Rebellion and committed to the Manitoba Asylum for the Insane in Selkirk. He escaped and sent a message through his sister to the prime minister of Canada: "If you hang Riel you will provoke a more dangerous and attrocious [sic] outbreak. He is the sole mouthpiece of the aborigines and must be heard. Let him free and I am willing to be shot in his place." This desperate plea, of course, came to nothing.

An angry conflict flared up between English and French Canadians. Ontarians rejoiced that Riel was to be hanged. But according to the Quebec papers, every Frenchman wanted Riel to be pardoned.

Nothing more could be done, said Sir John A. Macdonald. Because there were some doubts about Riel's mental state, he added, three doctors had assessed Riel and all three insisted that he was sane. Riel was guilty of high treason, and there was no reason for delaying his execution a moment longer.

As prime minister, Sir John A. had the last word: "He will hang, though every dog in Quebec barks in his favour."

And hang he did. According to the *Quebec Daily Telegraph*, after Riel's arms were pinioned on the gallows on November 16, 1885, accompanied by Deputy Sheriff Gibson and fathers André and McWilliams, he "walked firmly and without assistance down the six steps to the scaffold, taking his stand on the drop, and constantly [repeating] in French: 'In God I put my trust.'" Two minutes after the lever was pulled, he was dead.

On the eve of his execution, Louis Riel said, "In a hundred years, they'll still be talking about me."

And we still are.

As the *Quebec Daily Telegraph* bleakly and presciently put it in the issue that appeared on the day Riel died:

> The wedge of discord has been, so to speak, driven deeply into the quivering flesh of the body politic, and Heaven only knows where the trouble will end. The execution of Riel marks the starting point on a very perilous path. With one portion of the Canadian population regarding the tragic event as the fit conclusion to a turbulent, murderous and rebellious career and the other portion viewing it as the martyrdom of a hero and a patriot, whose only crime was to have been of their blood and to have loved his poor downtrodden fellow-countrymen in the North West too well, it will be admitted, we think,

that the outlook for the future is not encouraging. A wound has been sustained that will rankle and fester for years to come.

Historians and political commentators have noted that the fault lines exposed by the rebellion and Riel's trial have indeed continued to divide Canada to this day: east versus west, English versus French, Native people versus the rest.

Sir John A. Macdonald would probably turn in his grave at the thought, but there are some eerie similarities between Louis Riel and Sir John A.'s good friend and fellow Father of Confederation Thomas D'Arcy McGee. Many people see Riel, too, as a Father of Confederation. After all, he did bring Manitoba into the Dominion of Canada. Both Riel and McGee were passionate speakers and visionaries, committed to the land they called home. Both had powerful enemies who plotted their downfall. And both of them died in their early forties, violently.

CHAPTER 7

The Petticoat and the Noose

She was small and slim, with a long, narrow face and dark curly hair reaching to her shoulders. She was just twenty-two years old, married, and living in the village of Blairmore in the Crowsnest Pass area of the Rocky Mountains. Her name was Florence Lassandro. And at just after six o'clock on May 2, 1923, as dawn was breaking in what witnesses described as a "fretful morning sky," she became the first, and last, woman to ever be hanged in Alberta. She died with the words "I forgive everybody" on her lips.

From around 1916 to 1923, it was like the Wild West in Alberta. Those were the dark and desperate days of Prohibition. In the United States, the manufacture, transportation, importation, and sale of alcohol were completely banned. In less restrictive Canada, the provinces generally prohibited the sale, possession, and public consumption of alcohol, but there was no ban on the manufacture of liquor for export. This was a huge opportunity for entrepreneurial types wanting to make a quick buck. Heavily armed outlaws called bootleggers or rum-runners loaded their trucks and automobiles with crates of illegal booze and ran them across provincial and national borders to quench the public's thirst for hard liquor.

The most notorious bootlegger in the southwest corner of Alberta was a man called Emilio Picariello, also known as Pic, Emperor Pic, or the "King of the Crowsnest Pass." Emperor Pic owned a hotel and garage in Blairmore and was a member of the town council. Folks saw him as a gallant Robin Hood figure who put on free movies for poor kids. But these generous deeds became a front for his much more profitable — and sinister — criminal activities. He owned a fleet of speedy McLaughlin Buick automobiles, known as "Whiskey Sixes," which easily outran the sluggish Model T Fords of the Alberta Provincial Police. He demanded respect and loyalty from his employees, including Charles Lassandro, his chief mechanic, and Charles's much younger wife, Florence. Like Picariello, both of them were Italian immigrants.

Florence Lassandro loved the thrill of running booze across the British Columbia–Alberta border or over the foothills into Montana. And she came prepared, toting a .38 revolver in her purse. The guys liked having her on board. They felt the cops would be less likely to shoot if they saw a woman in the car.

Florence often rode shotgun for Pic's sixteen-year-old son, Steve. She was not in the car with him, though, on September 21, 1922. On that day, a constable with the Alberta Provincial Police, Steven Lawson, fired at Steve's liquor-laden automobile as it tore through the Crowsnest Pass town of Coleman after an abortive attempt to deliver a shipment to Pic's hotel in Blairmore.

Steve ended up with an injury to his hand, either from a bullet or from jamming it in the car door in his haste to decamp. Confused reports of the incident sent Picariello into a fury. "If he has shot my boy, I will kill him tonight, by God!" Grabbing a gun and picking up Florence on the way out of town, he raced over to Coleman to deal with Constable Lawson. At the end of the confrontation, the officer lay dead, a bullet in his back.

At first, as noted by anthropologist Ann Chandler in her article "The Lady & the Bootlegger," Florence was quite casual about the whole affair. "He's dead and I'm alive, and that's all there is to it," she reportedly said to the officers who arrested her. She also confessed to shooting Lawson.

Lawson's widow had been a horrified witness to her husband's violent death, and she broke down completely while testifying at Picariello and Lassandro's preliminary hearing. But it was the evidence of Pearl,

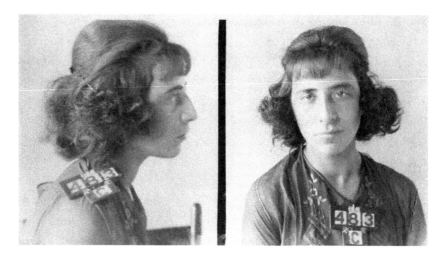

Bootlegger Florence Lassandro at the time of her arrest in 1922. She was executed in May 1923 for shooting a police officer and died with the words "I forgive everybody" on her lips.

Lawson's nine-year-old daughter, at their joint trial that stamped their death warrant. This was part of the recorded conversation in court between Pearl and an examining lawyer:

> "Daddy was standing at the car … he just put his arms around Pick's [sic] neck and Pick fired and daddy let go…. He dropped down."
>
> "Do you know why he dropped down. Do you, Pearlie?"
>
> "Because he was dead."
>
> "Who killed him, do you know?"
>
> "Pick and the lady."

The trial lasted a week. The jury found both defendants guilty, and Judge William Walsh sentenced them to death.

As the date of the execution approached, Florence had second thoughts about her confession. In a telegram to the minister of justice, she wrote: "I told Harris, my first solicitor, that I had agreed to take all blame." She claimed that Picariello had instructed her to "tell anyone who asks you that you did it."

Maybe Florence did take the rap for the murder to save her boss, believing that they would both escape the death penalty. Wasn't it true, after all, that women were never hanged in Canada? If that was the plan, it backfired. Badly. In spite of public objections and protests from the Canadian Prisoners' Welfare Association, Picariello and Lassandro's sentences were upheld.

Florence Lassandro went to the gallows, but the truth is that when it came to hanging in Canada, you really were better off being a woman than a man. It's all there in the numbers — 1,533 people were sentenced to death between 1867 and 1976, and just 58 of them were women. And of the 704 people actually hanged during that period, only 11 were women.

One of the reasons for this difference, according to researchers F. Murray Greenwood and Beverley Boissery in *Uncertain Justice: Canadian Women and Capital Punishment 1754–1953*, is that women were less likely to use potentially lethal tools like guns or axes or hammers, and thus less likely to commit violent crimes. There were always exceptions, of course, as in the case of Phoebe Campbell of Thorndale, Ontario. Phoebe claimed that two men with blackened faces had burst into the family's log cabin on July 15, 1871, demanding money. They attempted to shoot her husband, George, and when the gun misfired, they brutally hacked him to death with a knife and an axe. On the strength of her testimony, six local men were arrested, but questions soon arose as to the accuracy of Phoebe's story. Police investigations revealed that Phoebe had killed her husband to cover up her affair with a local workman, Thomas Coyle. She was arrested, tried, and convicted of murder.

Phoebe had three strikes against her: in addition to using deadly weapons to commit her crime, she was an adulterer and a husband killer. This type of offender often ended up on the gallows. As criminologist Sylvie Frigon points out, women were "punished for having stepped out of their social norms as women, wives, and mothers." The *London Free Press* referred to Campbell in August 1871 as "the most atrocious criminal of our century." Hanged in June 1872, she has gone down in history as the first woman to be executed in the Dominion of Canada.

An undated handwritten sheriff and doctor's report after the hanging of Phoebe Campbell in June 1872. She was the first woman to be executed in the Dominion of Canada.

Just one year later, Elizabeth Workman was also hanged for murdering her husband. It was well known in Mooretown, Ontario, that James Workman was a drunk who beat up his wife and stole the pittance she earned doing laundry and cleaning house for neighbours and local businesses. None of these details came up at Elizabeth's trial, where the judge, Adam Wilson, saw things differently. In his closing statement, he described Elizabeth to the jury as an unfaithful, sadistic woman who had tied up her husband and battered him with a mop handle for hours, finally killing him. Her inexperienced lawyer, John A. Mackenzie, appointed the day before the case began, was no match for the hostile judge. The jury convicted Elizabeth of murder, although they did recommend mercy and asked for her sentence to be commuted to life imprisonment.

There was a huge public outcry against her sentence. All in vain. In spite of the jury's recommendation, a flood of telegrams, five petitions (including one to the Governor General from 118 people in the Mooretown area), and two letters to the Department of Justice from Alexander Mackenzie, the future prime minister, Elizabeth Workman was hanged in June 1873.

One factor that should have helped Elizabeth avoid the noose — but didn't — was the unwillingness of officials in post-Confederation Canada to sentence women to death. Everyone in the criminal justice system was a man. Policemen, judges, lawyers, jurors, and politicians all firmly believed in the idea of chivalry: women in general should be respected and protected, and women offenders treated leniently.

Those involved in the system struggled to find the balance between protecting what they perceived to be the weaker sex and punishing those few vicious individuals who strayed outside the norms. This tension was again illustrated when the case of Angelina Napolitano came to court in May 1911. On Easter Sunday of that year, Angelina, twenty-eight years old and heavily pregnant, took an axe to her husband, Pietro.

As she afterwards explained in "her own hesitant and broken speech" to Honor D. Fanning of the *Pittsburgh Press*, "I was afraid. I felt hot. He went upstairs to bed. That was noon. The children were out at play. I was mad. Blood was hot. No place for me to go. No friends, I could not stand it. I was crazy. I go to the kitchen for the axe. I go upstairs. I think if he is awake he kill me. I did not care. I was sick of life. He was asleep. I struck him. I kill him. It had to be."

The facts emerged during Angelina's trial in Sault Ste. Marie. She and Pietro were both Italian immigrants who had arrived in Ontario in 1909. Her husband, a steel mill worker, started pressing her to earn more money for the family through prostitution. Angelina, a mother of four, refused. Pietro became increasingly insistent and increasingly violent. His wife was hospitalized after he attacked her viciously in November

1910, slashing her nine times on her head and shoulders. On the day of the murder, he had again threatened to kill her.

Her lawyer, appointed after trial proceedings had already begun, argued that her actions were driven by her husband's abuse and made reference to the stabbing in 1910. Interestingly, this was the first time that the battered woman defence was ever used in a Canadian court. The judge was not impressed: if everyone were to use an old injury to justify murder, he ruled, chaos would ensue. Angelina was sentenced to hang in August, which would allow just enough time for her baby to be born.

Public reaction was huge and immediate. Some argued that the murder proved that foreigners were a danger to the country, especially hot-blooded ones who were only too ready to resort to violence to settle their differences. But masses of people leapt to Angelina's defence, as the *Norwalk Hour* reported in July 1911: "Hundreds of thousands of men and women are petitioning against the death penalty in this case.… In Ottawa, Minister of Justice Aylesworth … is deluged daily with petitions pleading for her pardon. From every province of Canada, from every state in the American union, from the kingdoms over the sea, men and women are writing urging mercy."

Dr. Alexander Aalto, a middle-aged bachelor from Ashtabula, Ohio, offered to take Angelina's place on the gallows. And, according to an article in the *Reading Eagle*, so did Claude Winsby, an artist from Fort Scott, Kansas: "My desire is to offer my life as a substitute for one which is capable of bringing into the world a child, which, if in this country, might rise to the head of the nation. In America we esteem a pure woman. In your country, if reports are true, you hang them for defending their chastity."

What a huge black eye for the Canadian criminal justice system.

Also stepping up to defend Angelina was the *Common Cause*, a British publication that styled itself as the organ of the National Union of Women's Suffrage Societies: "We imagine that the sentence will not be carried out. But what decent purpose could be served by passing sentence of death upon a pregnant woman? What fantastic notions of the 'sacredness of life' can men have who will perform such monstrosities in the name of justice?"

Those men were listening. On July 14, 1911, the federal Cabinet commuted Angelina's sentence to life imprisonment. After eleven years in the Kingston Penitentiary, she was granted parole.

As Sir Wilfrid Laurier summed it up in the House of Commons in 1917, there was "something revolting in the idea that a woman should be sentenced to death."

But by the time Florence Lassandro committed her crime in 1922, things were changing in Canada and across the world. Women were on the move. They were marching, waving banners, organizing protests. They resented being treated as inferior to men. They campaigned for the right to vote in public elections and take part in political life. And, in addition to demanding the same opportunities as men, women were prepared to accept the same responsibilities.

In sentencing Florence to death, Judge William Walsh said: "The only thing that can be said in favour of the prisoner, Lassandro, is that she is a woman. I know, of course, quite well the reluctance that there is to execute the death sentence upon a woman.... If she was a man, there could be no question but that the sentence should be executed."

The letters and petitions for and against commuting Florence Lassandro's death sentence to life in prison piled up. The outspoken Emily Murphy, Canada's first female magistrate, stressed her own opinion in a letter to Prime Minister William Lyon Mackenzie King: "I also desire to protest against the pernicious doctrine that because a person who commits a murder is a woman that person should escape from capital punishment. As women we claim the privileges of citizenship for our sex, and we accordingly are prepared to take upon ourselves the weight of the penalties as well."

As you can imagine, Emily Murphy's objection did not help Florence's cause.

What a difference a decade made. The same voices that had militantly supported Angelina against a male-dominated legal system were the undoing of Florence when women started pushing their way into the political arena.

But there were so many black marks against Florence that even the most passionate support from the women's movement would probably not have made the slightest difference. As noted by Jana Pruden in the *Edmonton Journal*, Florence packed a gun. She took part in the violent and criminal act of bootlegging. She shot a policeman in front of his family, which many saw as the wicked act of an ungrateful immigrant.

Emilio Picariello was hanged at the Provincial Gaol, Fort Saskatchewan, on May 2, 1923. Then Florence Lassandro, her senses dulled by a combination of alcohol and morphine, followed her boss up the eighteen steps to the scaffold. And she, too, dropped to her death.

Coincidentally, thirty years later, the eleventh and last woman to hang, Marguerite Pitre, also went to the gallows for helping a man commit a murder. Albert Guay wanted to get rid of his wife and marry his mistress. On his instructions, Marguerite bought dynamite that was used to make a time bomb, which was then planted on an airplane. The bomb exploded, punching the plane out of the sky. Mrs. Guay was on that flight, and she perished. So did twenty-two other passengers and crew members.

CHAPTER 8

The Science and Art of Hanging

William Marwood, the British executioner who trained John Radclive, has been credited with introducing to his native country the long drop method, which determined the length of rope required for a hanging. A cobbler by trade, Marwood must have been a very convincing salesman. He persuaded the authorities at Lincoln Castle's prison to let him try out this new technique to hang William Frederick Horry in 1872. The execution went off perfectly, launching fifty-four-year-old Marwood's new career as official hangman.

The long drop, also known as the measured drop, was designed to break the prisoner's neck instead of causing death by strangulation. Within a few years, this method, originally developed by doctors in Ireland, entirely replaced the existing types of hanging: the short drop, where the condemned person would fall just a few inches and strangle to death, and the standard drop, where the individual would fall between four and six feet and break his or her neck (or, if that failed, die more slowly of strangulation).

The advantage of the long drop was that it was based on scientific principles. A mathematical formula, predicated on the height and body weight of the condemned, was used to calculate the distance of the drop after the trap was opened. The aim was to get the person falling quickly enough to provide a striking force (or drop energy) of between 840 and

1,260 foot-pounds. The placement of the knot of the noose just under the left ear was also a critical element in the process of dislocation or separation of the upper vertebrae. If everything went smoothly, it all made for a much quicker and presumably more humane death than strangulation.

Just in case the finer details of mathematical calculation left puzzled hangmen scratching their heads, British authorities published (and occasionally revised) an official table of drops, which was adopted in Canada as well.

But there was another crucial factor required to ensure a decent hanging: experience. To illustrate this point, Albert Pierrepoint, pre-eminent British hangman in the first half of the twentieth century, quoted in his autobiography *Executioner: Pierrepoint* the words of his first instructor: "Now you've got your table, Home Office issue, table of drops, executioners, for the use of. Use it, but use your own judgement too. Remember it's only a guide, and you've got to vary it according to your experience.... An executioner has to use his own judgement. That only comes by experience."

So instead of the previous one-size-fits-all approach, you had a new and humane method of calculating the drop, tailored to the individual. In addition, the hangman was a professional, a craftsman who could fall back on his training and experience to fine-tune his calculations.

Science plus art. What could possibly go wrong?

As it turns out, quite a lot.

Your executioner, for example, might miscalculate the drop, making it too short. On December 15, 1870, the *Morning Chronicle* reported on the double hanging at the Frontenac County Gaol in Kingston, Ontario, of Daniel Mann, convicted for the murder of a prison guard at the Kingston Penitentiary, and John Deacon, convicted of poisoning his wife with a cup of arsenic-laced tea. There were two masked hangmen on duty that day, neither of them able to prevent what happened when the signal was given: "The drop fell with a great noise, the men falling about 5 feet; the fall was not sufficient to break either of their necks, so they died of strangulation.... It was ascertained from the Gaol Surgeon that Mann's pulse beat for ten minutes, and Deacon's for fifteen minutes."

Another possibility was that your executioner might miscalculate and make the drop too long. François Moreau, a thirty-seven-year-old farmer from St-Anaclet, Quebec, was hanged on January 13, 1882, for the axe murder of his wife, Démérise Roy. According to *Le Meutrier de Rimouski* (*The Murderer of Rimouski*), a report written at the time about the crime, trial, and execution of François Moreau, the drop was nine feet; death was instantaneous. Moreau's neck was broken, but his head was virtually separated from his body. It was a bloody scene, witnessed by the forty or so people who had permits to attend the hanging.

Or your executioner might try out something new, but not necessarily improved. John Radclive felt that he was making a significant contribution to the science of hanging with the development of his reverse hanging technique, which was also sometimes referred to as the "jerk 'em up" gallows. The difference from the traditional method was that the victim was launched into the air instead of being dropped through a trap door. It worked like this: a rope was thrown over the top beam of the scaffold. One end was tied around the neck of the accused and the other attached to a 350- or 400-pound iron weight. When the weight was dropped, the victim was yanked up into the air. A dislocated neck caused instantaneous death. That was the theory, anyway. It did not always work so well in practice.

As noted by Pfeifer and Leyton-Brown, Radclive employed this technique on a number of occasions in the early 1890s. In June 1890, he used it for one of the first hangings he performed in Canada. With disastrous results. He did not position wife-killer Henry Smith properly on the scaffold in London, Ontario. The man was pulled sideways instead of up into the air when the weight fell, making for a slow and horrifying death, and provoking howls of protest from the public. Despite this setback, Radclive persevered. Six days later, Peter Edwin Davis was executed in Belleville, Ontario, for the murder of his lover's husband; again, Radclive officiated, and again caused a drawn-out death by strangulation. According to one newspaper report, "the horrible spectacle made strong men turn pale and walk away." Another debacle was the hanging of Belleville resident James Kane, who murdered his wife in 1891. Kane's body spun around as it shot into the air, and he choked to death.

After a few more botched hangings, Radclive used this method for the last time when he hanged Robert Olsen in Dorchester, New

Brunswick, in 1892. Olsen made the fatal error of shooting a police officer in the course of a robbery attempt. This execution was a success, but, thereafter, Radclive quietly abandoned reverse hanging and reverted to the traditional trap door method. Another failed experiment.

An additional problem associated with hangings was equipment malfunction, often something so basic that a splash of lubricating oil could have fixed it. Reuse and recycle are perhaps not such good ideas when you're dealing with second-hand hanging apparatus. The scaffold brought into service in 1876 when John Young was hanged at Cayuga, Ontario, had last been used twenty years previously. When the deputy sheriff gave the nod for the hangman to pull the lever, the hinge on the trap door stuck fast. Young was forced to wait for three or four minutes, kneeling on the trap door with a white hood over his head while a constable dashed into the jail to fetch a hammer. With a few mighty thwacks, the hangman unjammed the hinge, sending Young to his death. Understandably, as the *Toronto Globe* reported, "this untoward accident caused a thrill of horror to pass through the hearts of all those who witnessed it."

A common error, especially among less experienced hangmen, was positioning the knot incorrectly, which is what happened in November 1889 when William Harvey was hanged in Guelph, Ontario. Harvey, described as fifty-five or sixty years old with large, cloudy eyes, a grey beard, and a gentlemanly appearance, seemed such an unlikely perpetrator of the terrible crimes he committed. After being fired for embezzling $4,000 from his employer, he bought a revolver and shot his wife and two daughters to save them from the taint of his actions. Only prompt intervention by the police saved his son from the same fate.

Harvey's execution, as reported by the *Ottawa Daily Citizen*, was "a bungle all through." After the hanging, the distressed doctor on duty said that death had occurred after prolonged strangulation. He showed a reporter what the novice hangman had done. Instead of positioning the noose around the throat, he had placed it on the tip of the chin, with the knot pressing on the cheek, thus causing "unnecessary suffering and criminal torture." The hangman fled. Jurors at the inquest that followed were highly critical of his performance and recommended that "the government be asked to consider the advisability of employing an official expert executioner."

And what would happen if your first choice of executioner were not available? Nor, for that matter, your second choice?

Take the case of Garry Richard Barrett, who was hanged in July 1909 for the murder of a deputy warden at Edmonton's Alberta Penitentiary. Sheriff Robertson originally announced that John Radclive would officiate at the hanging, but then changed his story — Jack Holmes, a Regina-based hangman, would be in charge. Newsmen covering the execution were skeptical, as neither Radclive nor Holmes had been spotted in town. Further, according to an *Edmonton Journal* reporter who attended the hanging, "It is pointed out that although the executioner wore a mask and false moustache, he strongly resembled one of the guards as near as could be determined from a partial facial view."

The masked man's shoes, though, were in full view, and they were a dead giveaway: solid, brown, regulation-issue prison guard's shoes.

This was the second time that Barrett, a man with a long history of rage and other serious psychological problems, had flirted with the noose. The first time was in October 1907 when he attempted to shoot his common-law wife. His ten-year-old stepson hurled himself in front of his mother and took the bullet instead. Some argued that it was the boy's subsequent medical mistreatment rather than his injury that caused his death. Petitions flew, and Barrett's death sentence was commuted to life in prison.

But when Barrett stepped behind Richard Stedman, the deputy warden of the Alberta Penitentiary, in the prison carpentry shop and felled him with a single axe blow ("I wouldn't have done it if the deputy warden had let me see the doctor"), there was no second chance for him. He was tried three weeks later, and the jury took just five minutes to come back with a guilty verdict.

The prison guard/hangman, whether by accident or design, disastrously bungled the hanging. He positioned the noose incorrectly and nearly pulled the pin on the trap door too early, which would have sent the priest rather than the prisoner tumbling through the hole. Once the trap was sprung, the hangman twice tried to cut Barrett down. And twice the doctor on duty had to intervene, as Barrett was not yet dead. He died slowly of strangulation.

It happened on at least one more occasion that neither the first nor the second choice of executioner was available, and the third choice was incompetent, or perhaps drunk. To illustrate, look no further than the ghastly comedy of errors that saw Bennie Swim hanged twice in 1922.

In a classic tale of passion, jealousy, and murder, a young woman dumped her lover and married an older, dashing war hero. (Well, maybe not entirely classic — the woman and her lover were cousins.) The lover, Bennie Swim, traded some clothing and a rifle for a revolver, which he then used to shoot the war veteran, Harvey Trenholme, and then the new bride, Olive Swim Trenholme, in Benton Ridge, New Brunswick.

Bennie Swim knew he would hang for it, and he did.

Albion Foster, high sheriff of Carleton County, singled out Canada's busiest executioner, Arthur Ellis, as his first choice of hangman. But a two-month delay pending the results of Swim's psychiatric examination meant that Ellis had to withdraw. The sheriff then tried to secure the services of Jack Holmes, but Holmes was sidelined by an accident. Just imagine the sheriff's panic at this stage. Would he have to do the deed himself? To his relief, the sheriff of Montreal came to the rescue, recommending for the job a man named M.A. Doyle. Just to be safe, Foster hired F.G. Gill as a backup. Both men travelled to Woodstock, New Brunswick, to officiate.

Swim was hanged just after 5:00 a.m. on October 6, 1922. After a few minutes, he was examined by the three doctors in attendance and the order was given to cut him down. But to the consternation of the doctors and the eighteen others who attended the hanging, Swim had survived. He was breathing, and over the next thirty minutes, his pulse became stronger.

Faced with this hideous dilemma, the lawmen in charge decided to follow the letter of the law: to hang Swim by the neck until he was dead. So the unconscious man was carried back to the gallows and hanged again, this time by Gill. And this time, there was no mistake. But more than three-quarters of an hour had elapsed between the first and second hanging.

A commission of inquiry was launched to address the rumours swirling around the case: that hangman Doyle was disrespectful and drunk and gave the order to cut Swim down prematurely.

The commissioner, J. Dickson, was very critical of Doyle's performance. And he ended his report with a withering condemnation of Canada's system of capital punishment and the dreadful burden it placed on the sheriff: "The sentence of the court is that the prisoner be hanged by the neck until he is dead. The duty of carrying out this sentence is placed on the sheriff. He receives no instructions from any official source as to how the details of this gruesome task are to be carried out.... The wonder is that there are not more affairs of this nature."

The reality is that probably many more bungles of this nature occurred than were reported. Leyton-Brown estimates that between one-third and two-thirds of Canadian hangings were botched. And over time, the public began to view strangulation itself as a type of failure. Observers and reporters reacted with shock and horror ("Revolting Scene at Execution" was a typical headline), but the authorities were not always keen to acknowledge errors or inadequacies. Not only did they start trying to keep details of substandard hangings out of the public eye, but they also became reluctant to report problems to their superiors. For example, Sheriff Robertson, the man in charge of the horribly mismanaged hanging of warden-killer Barrett in Edmonton, calmly telegraphed the Canadian undersecretary of state in Ottawa to let him know that "the execution of Garry R. Barrett [has] taken place without a hitch at 6.48 this morning."

Albert Pierrepoint, arguably the most proficient of British executioners, described hanging in his memoirs as "quick, certain, and humane." He claimed that he had never bungled an execution and that the longest time he had ever taken to do the job was between twenty and twenty-five seconds. Arthur Ellis, arguably the most prolific and capable of Canadian executioners, was also proud of his achievements and enjoyed trumpeting them to the world. As he told *The Globe* in 1912: "I have never had a bungle, and consider I am rendering a service to society by despatching those unfortunates in the most humane way possible." He spoke too soon. After what a newspaper referred to as "one or two 'accidents' out west," a dreadful miscalculation in 1935 would make a mockery of his words.

CHAPTER 9

Arthur Ellis:
Canada's Most Famous Hangman

Alexander Armstrong English, also known as Arthur Bartholomew Alexander English, but best known as Arthur Ellis, had a violent job. He was also a violent man.

By the time executioner John Radclive retired in 1910, the Canadian government had already found a "pro" to take his place. According to one source, Prime Minister Wilfrid Laurier had penned a letter to the Home Office in Britain, asking for recommendations, and the name of ex-army officer Alexander English floated to the top. English moved to Montreal, Quebec, and became the busiest executioner in Canadian history. He used the professional name of Arthur Ellis after a famous English hangman named John Ellis, who he claimed was an uncle.

Ellis quickly settled into his new life in Canada. One of his first jobs was the hanging of Pasquale Ventricini in Toronto, Ontario, in June 1910. Ventricini had come to Canada from Italy to build a better life for his wife and children. Those dreams came crashing down during a drunken brawl in March 1910, when he stabbed his friend Raffael Fabbio to death. A jury found Ventricini guilty of murder, although they did make a recommendation for mercy. But their argument that "the man was a foreigner and not used to Canadian ways" did not make much of an impression on Judge Riddell, and Ventricini went to the gallows. Arthur Ellis carried out the hanging at Toronto's notorious Don Jail.

For the next twenty-five years, Ellis's duties took him all over Canada, from Halifax to Vancouver. In 1920, he hanged John Wilson, an ex–Royal North-West Mounted Police officer convicted of killing his wife, at the Prince Albert Jail in Saskatoon, Saskatchewan. This was an unusual case in that it was the only time in Canadian history that a police officer was hanged for his crime.

One of Ellis's most important assignments was the quadruple hanging of members of the eight-man Hochelaga Gang in 1924.

On April 1 of that year, a Hochelaga Bank payroll car was held up in Montreal, and the driver was murdered. The criminals made off with around $140,000, but they were soon apprehended and brought to trial. The case sparked a huge amount of public interest, as among the accused were gang leader Tony Frank, known as "King of the Underworld," and Louis Morel, a former detective with the city of Montreal. The gangsters received the death penalty. The night before they were hanged, the police were out in force inside and around the Bordeaux jail, on the alert for any escape attempts. Crowds turned up before dawn and lined the streets to catch a glimpse of the sensational and very rare execution of four men simultaneously.

Another high-profile hanging that came Ellis's way was that of Earle Leonard Nelson in 1927. Ellis reportedly told the press that he was "delighted to perform" the execution. Nelson was an American serial killer also known as the Dark Strangler (because of his swarthy skin) or the Gorilla Killer (because of his huge hands and bestial attacks). He began committing sex crimes in 1918, when he was twenty-one years old, but he hit his stride in 1926, murdering and then sexually molesting more than twenty women and girls in the United States and, later, two in Canada. His killing frenzy finally ended in Winnipeg, Manitoba, where he met his demise at the end of a rope.

Although hangman Ellis complained bitterly in 1912 about not receiving any stipend from the government, by 1935, as reported in the *Sunday Spartanburg Herald-Journal*, he was being paid a yearly salary in Quebec for taking care of all hangings in the province. Throughout the rest of Canada, each job would earn him between $150 and $200 plus expenses. He travelled with his ropes, straps, and a black cap packed into a black bag. When he journeyed to smaller centres where there were no permanent gallows, he would take along his own portable kit, painted a dazzling red.

Before his death in 1938, Ellis claimed to have carried out more than six hundred hangings in England, the Middle East, and Canada. It's impossible to verify whether his tally was quite this high, as record-keeping was not entirely reliable in the first few decades of the twentieth century, and the pseudonym of Arthur Ellis was commonly used by other Canadian executioners.

An old photo of Ellis, dated 1925, shows a man with deeply furrowed cheeks and small, pebble-shaped glasses. His working outfit was a frock coat and striped trousers, and he would often pin a flower to his lapel. He did not hide his identity; in fact, he enjoyed telling people who he was and what he did for a living — especially if they offered him a drink.

Ellis knew that the relationship between the executioner and the public was a very complicated one. "Who put me where I am?" he once asked an interviewer. "Surely it was yourself and the other citizens of this country!"

Some newspapers of the day tried to accentuate Ellis's human side. "Hangman Ellis Keen Soccer Fan When He Isn't Handling Noose" gushed a 1933 report in the *Drummondville Spokesman*, painting a rosy picture of a concerned citizen buying uniforms and organizing football clubs for Montreal youth. He was kindly "Uncle Arthur" to a ten-year-old girl, advising her on how to save up to buy a buffalo ranch out west.

Ellis, too, liked to emphasize his humanity. "I always smile at a hanging," he told reporters. "Do you realize that my face is the last living thing the murderer sees before he dies? I try to make his last moments as pleasant as possible."

But Ellis's self-destructiveness and violence always bubbled close to the surface. He was armed and dangerous, often carrying a .38 revolver stuck into his belt. Like John Radclive before him, he was said to be a heavy drinker. The *Montreal Daily Mail* reported in January 1914 that hangman Ellis had been convicted of carrying a loaded revolver and of being drunk. He was fined $5 for the first charge and given a suspended sentence for the second.

Ellis was well known to the police in Montreal, who once arrested him for beating and attempting to strangle his wife, Edith Grimsdale. It is said that he avoided a trial simply because there were three convicted men awaiting execution in Vancouver.

Whether this particular story is true or not, what is completely without doubt is that Ellis had a hectic schedule. "Canada Noose Adjuster Busy," explained the *Milwaukee Sentinel* in January 1926. "Executions throughout the dominion are keeping Hangman Arthur Ellis on the jump. He has seven engagements from Halifax to Vancouver up to Feb. 5, and four sheriffs have asked him to keep open four dates in February."

Ellis was proud of his speed and skill on the job. Sometimes he would hand a stopwatch to a newsman at a hanging and ask him to check out his efficiency.

"But how do you know what the condemned man will weigh?" a lawyer once asked him in a conversation recorded by B.C. reporter Bruce Alistair "Pinkie" McKelvie.

"I take a look at him in his cell. I can tell to within a fraction of a pound his weight after one glance. You see, the length of the drop depends upon the weight of the subject."

And calculating the length of rope correctly was crucial to the success of the hanging — too short a drop and the individual might be strangled; too long, decapitated.

Of course, mistakes did sometimes happen.

Take the case of Antonio Sprecarce in 1919, for example. Sprecarce was, by all accounts, a nasty piece of work who had been involved in several shooting incidents and run-ins with the police. After being fired from his job at the Grand Trunk Railway in Montreal, he returned to the railroad yards to demand his job back, as well as some pay he claimed was owed to him. In a subsequent clash with his ex-foreman, Sprecarce pulled out a gun and, as multiple witnesses testified at his trial, pumped several bullets into the man. It was an open-and-shut case; the jury took just five minutes to find him guilty.

It took Sprecarce a lot longer to die.

Always a lightweight, he lost around twelve pounds while in prison. This does not seem to have been factored into Ellis's mathematical calculations when he officiated at Sprecarce's hanging. The drop was much too short, and Sprecarce's neck was not broken when the trap was sprung. He was cut down and lay there in full view of onlookers, taking more than an hour to die.

Quite the reverse was the hanging of Daniel Prockiw of Winnipeg in 1926. Prockiw weighed in at 240 pounds. He was sentenced to hang for the murder of Annie Cardno, his common-law wife. Prockiw was every hangman's nightmare — a big man with a thin neck. Ellis was worried as he prepared for the hanging, and rightly so. It ended up being horribly bungled. The drop was too long, and Prockiw's head was literally torn from his body.

Were these bungled jobs the result of gross incompetence, or were some hangings simply impossible to carry out effectively? Hard to tell, although Ellis never hesitated to make his own viewpoint known. As he wrote in a letter to Sheriff Lawreason of Hamilton, Ontario: "No one has suffered more than I have when I have had to use antiquated conditions and expected to give something that was impossible under the conditions that exist."

Never was this more chillingly illustrated than with the 1935 hanging of Tommasina Teolis of Montreal.

Teolis had come up with a brilliant way to extricate herself from her unhappy marriage. She hired a hit man, Leone Gagliardi, to bump off her husband, Nicholas Sarao, offering Gagliardi a cut of Sarao's $5,000 life insurance policy. Gagliardi invited so-called "high school gangster" Angelo Donafrio along for the ride. The two men lured Sarao to the Blue Bonnet Racetrack in Montreal, where they beat him to death. Grilled by police, Gagliardi confessed. Teolis and her accomplices were sentenced to death, and all three were led to the gallows at Montreal's Bordeaux jail on March 29, 1935. Arthur Ellis, master hangman, officiated.

The day began badly. Ellis had decided to hang the two men together; he had handled double, and even quadruple, hangings (like that of the Hochelaga Gang) with great competence in the past. Not this time. Neither man was killed by the drop; both died slowly of strangulation.

Then it was Teolis's turn. As usual, Ellis had gone to the jail the day before the hanging to examine Teolis and calculate the length of rope he

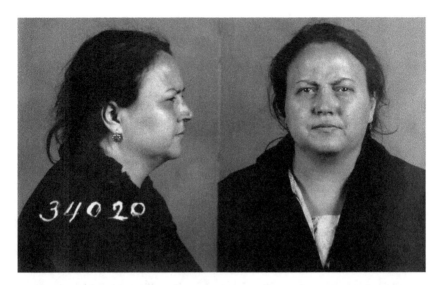

In March 1935, hangman Arthur Ellis miscalculated the length of rope required for the execution of husband killer Tommasina Teolis, and she was decapitated. This shocking event led to a huge public outcry and signalled the end of Ellis's career.

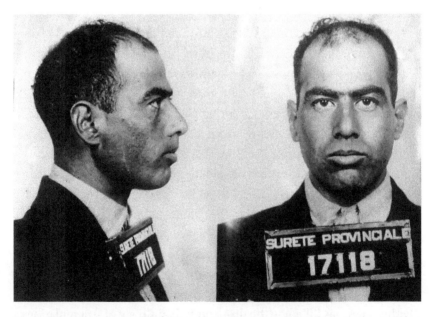

Leone Gagliardi was one of Tommasina Teolis's accomplices in the murder of her husband, Nicholas Sarao. Gagliardi confessed when questioned by the police, and he preceded Teolis to the gallows in March 1935.

would need. The authorities, he claimed, refused to let him see her and instead handed him a slip of paper giving her weight as 145 pounds. As it turned out, that was what she had weighed when she first went to prison. She was now nearly forty pounds heavier. Also, like Prockiw, Teolis had a weak neck.

What happened next once again highlighted the importance of calculating the length of the drop accurately. The rope used on March 29, 1935, was way, way too long, and Tommasina Teolis's head was severed from her body.

You may remember Sir Wilfrid Laurier's words in the House of Commons in 1917 that there was "something revolting in the idea that a woman should be sentenced to death." Well, if sentencing and hanging a woman was ungentlemanly and disgusting, beheading a woman was beyond repulsive.

The newspapers pounced on the gruesome story. "Head Torn From Body By Noose" was the headline in Windsor Ontario's *Border Cities*

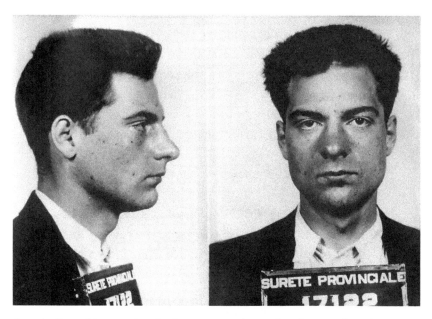

Angelo Donafrio was the third person implicated in the murder of Nicholas Sarao. He and Gagliardi were hanged together.

Star. "WOMAN KILLER DECAPITATED BY CANADIAN NOOSE," shrieked the *Miami News.*

"There is no earthly reason for such a thing to happen," said Teolis's attorney in a protest to the Department of Justice. "It was horrible."

The catastrophe put an end to the practice of allowing the public to get tickets to watch hangings. It also put an end to Arthur Ellis's career. He was never actually fired; instead, he was quietly boycotted. Sheriffs simply stopped sending him work.

In July 1938, the *Montreal Gazette* reported that Ellis, aged seventy-three, had been found starving in a Montreal rooming house and was near death in the Ste. Jeanne d'Arc Hospital. He was "penniless and alone after months of vain searching for some means of self-support," having subsisted since his ouster as hangman on handouts from friends.

Ellis died the following day of what was described as "a brief illness of undisclosed nature." Modern researchers say that his death was caused by an alcohol-related disease. Fewer than twenty people, most of them cops or newsmen, attended his funeral. And even though they had been separated for six years, his wife, Edith Grimsdale, was also there.

"He was a good man, a good man," she sobbed.

Newspaper reports published at that time suggest that "abusive," rather than "good," might have been a more accurate description of Ellis's husbandly behaviour.

Grimsdale survived her spouse by twenty-two years. Loyal to the end, she insisted on being buried alongside him in Montreal's Mount Royal Cemetery.

Today, Arthur Ellis is remembered in two ways — one public and one very private.

Every year, the Crime Writers of Canada celebrates the best of this country's crime and mystery writing. At a splendid gala, winners are presented with an Arthur Ellis Award, a wooden figure nicknamed "Arthur" with a noose around its neck that "dances" when you pull a string.

You will find the other memorial to Arthur Ellis in Section N of the Mount Royal Cemetery in Montreal. On a small mound with a backdrop of trees stands a simple headstone for Alexander A. English and Edith Grimsdale. And beneath their names, two words: AT REST.

CHAPTER 10

Reasonable Doubt

The sudden death in October 1883 of a young pregnant woman in Artemesia Township (near Owen Sound, Ontario) sent a shiver of shock and horror through the small farming community. Rosanna Leppard, aged twenty-five, had been married for just six weeks to fifty-five-year-old labourer Cook Teets when she became violently ill during the night. Within hours, she was dead. The doctor who performed the post-mortem was suspicious. So were the coroner and the twelve jurymen at the inquest that followed her death. Her symptoms — stomach pains and vomiting — strongly pointed to death by poisoning. The contents of her stomach were sent away to Toronto for analysis. The report that came back confirmed everyone's suspicions: Rosanna Leppard had died of strychnine poisoning. There was no evidence to show that she had committed suicide. "*No!*" thundered the *Markdale Standard* on November 22, 1883, "every fact seems to point to one of the most heartless, cold-blooded murders, having been committed in our neighbourhood, that has ever stained the annals of crime in our country."

But who committed it?

When the local policeman, Constable Fields, searched Teets's house, he found a half-filled bottle labelled STRYCHNINE — POISON. Fields also found a $4,500 insurance policy on Rosanna's life, payable to Teets in the event of her death.

"Follow the money!" is a common refrain in politics and police procedurals. In this case, the money trail led directly to Teets, the beneficiary of his wife's life insurance policy. He was arrested for murder, and he spent the next year locked up and awaiting trial in the Owen Sound Gaol.

Onlookers were shocked at the change in Teets's appearance when the case went to trial in November 1884. According to one news report, he had been clean-shaven and controlled at the coroner's inquest after his wife's death, with tightly compressed lips and an almost rigid expression on his face. Now, he was dishevelled, with a long flowing grey beard and a heavy moustache. Sweating profusely and breathing with difficulty, he seemed restless, uneasy, and in great pain.

According to the *Flesherton Advance*, the trial judge, Justice J.D. Armour, "charged very strongly against the prisoner but presented the facts clearly and fully." It took the jury thirty minutes to come to their verdict: Guilty. Although there was a request for mercy, the judge told Teets that he held out no hope for the success of any appeal. He was proven correct. In spite of petitions for clemency, Teets was hanged at dawn on December 5, 1884, the first person to meet his death at the Owen Sound Gaol.

An open-and-shut case, you might think. But it was much more complicated than that.

Cook Teets was completely blind. He had lost the sight in one eye as a youth after being struck by a rock-filled snowball, and the other through inflammation some years later. Even though he and Leppard were newly married, he was still living with his mother, while his wife and her two children from a previous marriage stayed with hers. The couple had been together the day before she died, but had parted around 5:00 p.m. According to the evidence, Teets was nowhere near his wife for a period of twelve or more hours before her death.

Teets made a statement to his lawyer the day before he was hanged, repeating the position he had taken since the beginning of the case.

Yes, he had had strychnine in his possession. But he used it to kill foxes, not people: "I do not know where the poison was got, or who got it. Wherever it came from it never came out of my bottle. I had the poison for not quite two years. I got it in Lexington, Michigan, for to get furs.

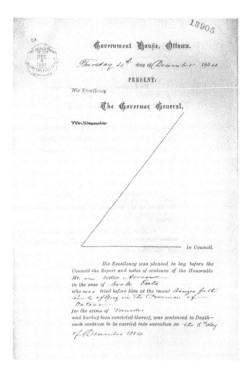

In spite of petitions from both residents of Grey County and members of the Ontario bar, an Order-in-Council dated December 4, 1884, directed that the hanging of Cook Teets should proceed the following day.

I used some of it, and got a few furs for a cape for my mother, which I tanned myself. I made no secret about having the poison."

Yes, he took out an insurance policy on his wife's life: "Shortly before our marriage, with the advice and consent of her father, I let her have money to insure her life.... It was at her own request that her life was insured. She wanted it in case anything happened to her that there would be something to support her children."

He died insisting that he was an innocent man.

Which he may well have been.

Even if Teets had the weapon (poison) and the motive (insurance money) to commit murder, where was the opportunity? Strychnine is known to be a foul-tasting, quick-acting poison. Symptoms can begin within minutes, and the victim will die two or three hours after exposure. A blind man would have had difficulty in administering such a poison without arousing suspicion in the first place, and Teets was nowhere near his wife during those crucial early morning hours when she must have swallowed the poison. Perhaps someone else had taken advantage of the situation? As the *Hanover Post* hinted darkly in an editorial after Teets's hanging: "We must admit that the fact of his having the strychnine and the policy were known to some person or persons, then how easy, with such a knowledge, for the person with malice and murderous intent to administer the strychnine and hang poor blind Cook Teets for the murder."

Suspicion fell on Rosanna Leppard's disreputable family and on her mother in particular. Roseanne O'Malley Leppard, a Catholic woman of Irish descent, consented to Rosanna and Teets's marriage and then hounded Teets to get it done as quickly as possible — perhaps because Rosanna was pregnant? But, according to Teets, O'Malley Leppard was enraged when the couple ran off to Toronto to wed. In his last statement, Teets claimed that his wife had told him about an exchange between her and her mother:

"Who were you married by — a [Catholic] priest?" her mother had asked.

"No, by a Presbyterian minister."

"Take him and go to hell with him, for that is where you will go any way."

Did her mother decide to hasten Rosanna's descent into hell? Teets also stated that his wife had said "her mother was illusing [*sic*] her," and that she wanted to move out of the parental home.

O'Malley Leppard certainly had the opportunity to murder her daughter. She was alone with Rosanna during her last meal and was with her when she died. She appeared at the coroner's inquest with a black eye, which she claimed occurred when her daughter had lashed out randomly in her death throes. But was Rosanna in actual fact striking out at the person she knew was her murderer? During the trial, the older woman was accused of scolding her daughter about the cost and inconvenience of having to keep her and her children. Ominously, witnesses claimed, O'Malley Leppard had been brandishing a poker at the time.

O'Malley Leppard was hardly a stable individual — she spent time in jail for attempting to burn down a neighbour's barn, and some years after Rosanna died, she was committed to the Toronto Asylum, possibly suffering from schizophrenia, and she remained institutionalized until her death in 1918.

Teets said unequivocally that his mother-in-law, who had testified both at the inquest and the trial, was a liar. She asked him for strychnine to poison dogs: "I never gave her any. I never suggested to her to put it in onions to poison people who were stealing her onions. That whole story is a fabrication."

No one witnessed the murder; it was Teets's word against the Leppard family's. Even at the time, many in the community believed in Teets's innocence. They claimed that he had been hanged on very flimsy circumstantial evidence.

As Chief Justice James Chalmers McRuer put it in his charge to the jury in the 1951 *Rex v. Sullivan* manslaughter case in Ottawa: "To find the accused guilty on circumstantial evidence, you must be convinced not only that the circumstances are consistent with the guilt of the accused, but that those circumstances are inconsistent with any other conclusion."

Were the circumstances in Teets's case consistent with his guilt and inconsistent with anyone else's? Many thought not.

— — —

What the *Montreal Gazette* in July 1931 called "the ever perplexing problem of circumstantial evidence" was also a key factor in the case of Abraham Steinberg, which took place in Toronto but enthralled the whole country for more than a year. Steinberg was accused of murdering his nephew and business partner, Samuel Goldberg. After two trials, appeals to the Supreme Court of Ontario, to the Supreme Court of Canada, and finally to the Governor-General-in-Council, and despite multiple petitions signed by more than thirty thousand people pleading for clemency and a personal appeal to the prime minister by the mayor of Toronto, Steinberg was hanged at the Don Jail on the morning of July 14, 1931.

The case started in vintage film noir style, with a dead man, a bullet hole through his skull, slumped over a desk in a burning building in downtown Toronto. On March 5, 1930, Sam Goldberg had been shot in his office at Goldberg Monument Works, and his corpse was set on fire to mask the murder.

The police became very interested in Steinberg, especially after they found his .38 revolver hidden in the company's yard the day after the shooting. As reported by *The Globe*, ballistics tests confirmed that the gun had fired what one expert called the "mortal bullet." Steinberg was arrested and charged with murder. It came out at the inquest that the partners had been quarrelling for months, and the police were convinced that they had their man.

At Steinberg's trial, the Crown focused on the ongoing clashes between Steinberg and Goldberg. They showed that the murder weapon belonged to Steinberg, although they couldn't prove that he had actually fired it. There were only four keys to the office. A witness had seen a man in a grey overcoat and cap take a key out of his pocket and unlock the office door. The prosecution claimed that this was Steinberg. The most damning evidence was provided by the star witness for the prosecution, James Creighton. He had been held at the Don Jail at the same time as Steinberg, facing charges of procuring false evidence in a lawsuit. Creighton swore that Steinberg had made a confession to him while they were both in prison.

The problem was, as pointed out by Susan McNicoll in *Toronto Murders: Mysteries, Crime, and Scandals*, that Steinberg had a solid alibi.

He had been visiting his friend Max Rotenberg at the time of the murder. Rotenberg and four other witnesses stated that Steinberg was wearing a blue coat and hat that evening. The defence's case was strong: the office door was always kept open when someone was inside, so why would anyone need to unlock it? And Creighton was totally unreliable, or, as counsel put it, "They could not hang a dog on the story told by that witness." Steinberg had tears in his eyes when the jury couldn't come to a verdict, and the judge ordered a new trial.

Blue coat, grey coat.

The difference between innocence and guilt can sometimes hang on such shreds of circumstantial evidence. And so it was with Steinberg. At his second trial, the prosecution produced a police witness who testified that Steinberg had been wearing a grey overcoat and cap when he was questioned at police headquarters on the night of the murder.

Friends and supporters were shocked that Steinberg's life depended on such shaky evidence — and on Creighton's testimony in particular. Steinberg spoke English with great difficulty and steadfastly denied his guilt even when subjected to gruelling police questioning — why would he confess to a total stranger? Further, the jury was totally unaware that Creighton had been a psychiatric patient and that the charges against him were dropped after he testified.

This time, Steinberg was found guilty. And early in the morning of July 15, 1931, a few curious bystanders gathered to read the notice posted on the door to the Don Jail: "Judgement of death was this day executed on Abraham Steinberg in the common jail of the County of York, at Toronto."

Again to quote Justice McRuer in *Rex v. Sullivan*: "The onus of proof in this case, as in every criminal case, is upon the Crown from the beginning to the end, to prove the accused guilty beyond a reasonable doubt." Reasonable doubt, passed along to Canada from English common law, is one of the underpinnings of the criminal justice system. It means that, based on reason and common sense, a person must be sure of the guilt of the accused.

In the case of both Teets and Steinberg, the Crown secured a guilty conviction and both men went to the gallows. But Teets could not have been the individual who fed quick-acting poison to his wife, and Steinberg had a rock-solid alibi for the time of his nephew's slaying. So *were* both men guilty beyond a reasonable doubt? Or were they actually found guilty of crimes they did not commit?

When the courts convict an innocent person today, the State can simply say sorry and award the wrongfully convicted both freedom and compensation for long years spent in prison. Or, as Crown prosecutor Michal Fairburn put it somewhat more elegantly in the Ontario Court of Appeal on October 15, 2007, when the court acquitted William Mullins-Johnson: "I wish to extend our sincere, profound and deepest apology to Mr. Mullins-Johnson and to his family for the miscarriage of justice that occurred." Mullins-Johnson had spent more than twelve years in prison for the rape and murder of his four-year-old niece, Valin. His conviction was partly based on a pathology report, which concluded that the child had been sexually molested and murdered. (One of the pathologists, Charles Smith, has since been completely discredited.) An investigation in 2005 by Chief Forensic Pathologist Michael Pollanen indicated that the signs that damned Mullins-Johnson were normal post-mortem occurrences, and that the child died of natural causes.

But once a person has been hanged, it's game over. Neither apologies nor restitution can ever make up for a gross miscarriage of justice. One of the most disturbing cases of this kind in the annals of Canadian criminal justice was that of Wilbert Coffin, prospector and woodsman, hanged in the beautiful and remote Gaspé Region of Quebec in 1956 for the murder of an American bear hunter.

CHAPTER 11

The Troubling Case of Wilbert Coffin

Mrs. Eugene Hunter Lindsey was wearing a trim grey suit and red hat when she took the stand in court that day. Her task was a grim one: to identify the personal effects of her husband and son at the murder trial of the Quebec native accused of killing her boy.

The Gaspé Peninsula or Gaspésie, in the southeast of the province of Quebec, juts out like a clenched fist into the Gulf of St. Lawrence. Nestled between the sea and the mountains, this vast region offers a multitude of year-round activities in stunningly beautiful natural settings. Dive into this unique experience, the travel guides tell you. And don't forget your camera.

But when Eugene Lindsey, a railroad steam fitter from Hollidaysburg, Pennsylvania, his seventeen-year-old son, Richard, and twenty-year-old family friend Frederick Claar packed up Lindsey's green 1947 pickup truck and set out for Gaspésie late on June 5, 1953, they did not have photo ops in mind. They were out to shoot them some bears — the bigger and blacker the better. Back then, this remote and rugged area was wildly popular with hunters from the States. Lindsey was familiar with the region and had indulged his passion for bear hunting in the Gaspé before. This brief visit was to celebrate Richard's high school graduation.

Mrs. Lindsey received a couple of postcards from her son. The second one, sent from the village of Gaspé and dated June 8, 1953, read in part: "Hi Mama.... We are ready to go into the woods tomorrow."

That was the last she ever heard from him.

On July 5, a month after the trio left home, Fred Claar's father became worried. The hunters had been due back by mid-June. Claar's concerned telephone calls touched off a search by the Quebec Provincial Police (QPP). The first thing the police located was Lindsey's truck, ominously abandoned in the bush about sixty miles from Gaspé village. On July 14 came an even more sinister discovery: the headless body of Eugene Lindsey, mangled and partially consumed, presumably by bears.

"Skeletal Parts Are Identified As the Remains of Elder Lindsey," announced the *Montreal Gazette* on July 23, 1953. According to the report, one official was convinced that Lindsey had been beaten with a rifle. He said that "bits of hair found on the rifle sight had minute pieces of skin attached, indicating Lindsey was clubbed over the head."

On that same day came another gruesome find: the bodies of Richard and Fred.

The grim discoveries continued to pile up. Near where the bodies were located, personal items belonging to the hunters were found strewn along a bush trail, some of them hanging from branches as if tossed from a moving vehicle. Eugene Lindsey was known to carry large sums of money. According to his widow, he had taken around $700 in cash on this trip. His empty wallet was found near the remains of his body.

Dr. Roussel, Quebec's medico-legal pathologist, couldn't determine the precise date each of them had perished or Eugene's exact cause of death, but he had no doubt that the two younger men had been shot. Richard Lindsey seemed to have been struck in the torso from behind. None of the three had fired a single bullet, but somebody else certainly had. Deep in the bush, the hunters had become the hunted.

This was murder.

And that was when thirty-eight-year-old Wilbert Coffin, outdoorsman, prospector, and resident of the small Quebec town of York Centre, stepped into the frame. He had offered his services when the call went out for volunteers to help find the three missing Americans. He told the police that he had met the hunters on June 10 and had even generously offered to assist them when their truck broke down. He was flagged as the last person to see the victims alive. Coffin's status as material witness

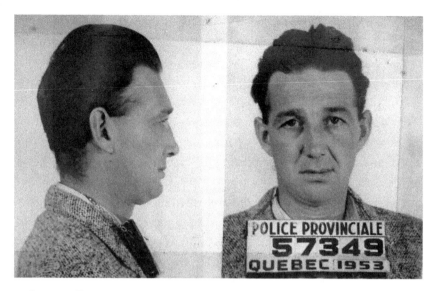

Wilbert Coffin at the time of his arrest in 1953. Coffin, a prospector and woodsman, was hanged in the beautiful Gaspé Region of Quebec in 1956 for the murder of an American bear hunter.

quickly moved to that of prime suspect, and on August 27, he was charged with murdering the two boys. He was eventually tried for one of the slayings — that of Richard Lindsey. The motive, according to the police, was robbery of cash and items such as a suitcase, a fuel pump, binoculars, towels, and trousers.

Coffin complained bitterly of his treatment at the hands of the QPP, led by Captain Alphonse Matte. He claimed to have been "railroaded" in an attempt to coerce him into confession. On one occasion, he was grilled for eighteen consecutive hours, and denied water and cigarettes. Marion Petrie, his common-law wife and the mother of his five-year-old son, was also treated harshly by the police. She was detained and questioned for eighteen hours. And as Coffin and Petrie were not legally married, she was forced to testify as a Crown witness at his trial, which spouses are normally exempt from doing.

Coffin's trial began on July 15, 1954 — almost exactly one year after the crime — at Percé, Quebec. On the prosecution side was the A-team of Paul Miquelon and Noel Dorion. They were two of Quebec's best-known prosecutors, with an impressive number of convictions under their respective belts. On the defence side was Raymond Maher, who introduced himself to Coffin's father as the best of the best. He would put a hundred witnesses on the stand, he said, to prove Coffin's innocence.

Eugene Lindsey's widow testified on the fourth day of the trial. She identified a stove and kerosene container as the equipment of the hunting party, as well as a watch, ring, belt, cap, a treasured knife, two torn undershirts, and a grey sweatshirt bearing the logo "Hollidaysburg Tigers," all of which had belonged to her son Richard. The sweatshirt, though, had not had a small, round hole in the logo when she'd packed it into her son's suitcase. That had been caused more recently, as the pathologist claimed, by the bullet that passed through his body.

Her voice faltered only once during the hour she spent on the witness stand. According to the *Pittsburgh Post-Gazette,* when she was asked if she recognized the handwriting on that postcard dated June 8, she replied with a sob: "I certainly do."

As the trial progressed, the prosecution's case became clear. They argued that Coffin had killed, then robbed, the trio. He'd spent substantial sums of money and had items belonging to the hunters in his possession at the time of his arrest. The evidence was all circumstantial. The murder weapon, for example, was never found. But the lawyers for the prosecution were very persuasive. They skilfully planted the perception that Coffin had borrowed a gun and called a witness who stated that he saw what looked like the barrel of a rifle sticking out of Coffin's truck. (Many months later, the witness recanted his trial testimony.)

As for the defence — well, there was none. When the time came for Maher to leap to his feet, produce his promised hundred witnesses, and definitively clear Coffin's name, he spoke just five words: "My Lord, the defence rests." He would not even allow Coffin to take the witness stand to tell his own story.

The jury was expecting a spirited defence. When that didn't materialize, what was left was a one-sided version of the events. At the end of the nineteen-day trial, it took the jury only thirty-four minutes to find Coffin guilty, and he was sentenced to hang at the Bordeaux jail in Montreal.

In the years since his conviction, much has been said and written about Coffin's defence, or lack thereof. Reckless and negligent in the extreme — that's how renowned Canadian defence lawyer Edward Greenspan, who studied the case, described Maher's performance. But, according to prominent Toronto criminal lawyer Arthur Maloney, Queen's Counsel (QC), the prosecution also played a role in denying Coffin a fair trial: "The defence was in many respects taken by surprise. Many witnesses were called, the nature or effect of whose testimony was unknown to the defence. This was improper and unfair."

But was Coffin guilty?

Of theft, certainly. He confessed as much, saying he had arranged with the hunters to go back to their truck a couple of days after his last contact with them. Finding the truck empty, he helped himself to some booze and got hammered in the process. His senses dulled by drink, he then helped himself to some of the hunters' belongings and decamped. It was just a tiny step, the Crown would have you believe, from this kind of petty pilfering to the worst kind of murder.

Coffin swore that he had no gun in his truck, as that witness for the prosecution had asserted. And the money, including U.S. dollars, that he was accused of spending? He drew up a list of people (including Lindsey) who had paid him, both before and after the period when the murder occurred, for staking mining claims and doing carpentry and other services for them.

With a death penalty looming, Coffin desperately needed legal help, which he obtained through the efforts of his own A-team: Quebec lawyer François de B. Gravel and Arthur Maloney QC. The affair stuttered on until February 1956. Coffin was reprieved seven times. Appeal followed appeal; rejection followed rejection; and telegrams and letters piled up. From this tangle of appeals and refusals, new strands of evidence emerged.

Early on, Coffin told police — a claim he held to steadfastly until his death — that when he last saw the victims, they were in the company of two other Americans. He described their vehicle as a jeep with yellow plywood sides. After the trial, several witnesses stepped forward to corroborate this story, among them a young Toronto doctor and his wife who had travelled across the St. Lawrence River by ferry on June 5, 1953.

They had noticed a jeep with a plywood cover that matched the description Coffin had given the QPP. There were two men in the vehicle, both wearing U.S. army–style jackets. Other witnesses also stated that a jeep with two occupants and U.S. licence plates was in the area around the time the murders were probably committed.

Another point: John Edward Belliveau, a journalist for the *Toronto Daily Star*, wrote a book about the case that was published after Coffin's death. According to Belliveau, something that did not come out at Coffin's trial was that Eugene Lindsey was reputed to be a hard-nosed moneylender, not above getting his enforcers to beat up his debtors, or doing the job with his own fists. Could Lindsey's enemies have followed him to the Gaspé and murdered him?

This jumble of contradictory information added up to just one word — *doubt*. As the *Ottawa Citizen* put it in October 1955: "Altogether the doubts raised in the public mind by Coffin's defence can hardly be allayed unless Ottawa orders a new trial, clear of wrangling about the conduct of the first trial and open to the introduction of any new evidence. This would seem the best way to determine Coffin's guilt or innocence, for where a man's life is at stake, the fullest resources of judicial procedure should be exhausted before inflicting the penalty."

Hopes were raised at the eleventh hour when the Supreme Court of Canada rejected Coffin's appeal by a vote of five to two. That may seem negative, but in the past, a divided vote had always resulted in commutation of the death sentence. This time, when relations between the provincial government of Quebec and the federal government in Ottawa were particularly strained, it did not. Quebec premier Maurice Duplessis was furious at the actions of the federally appointed Supreme Court; he complained that the feds were stomping on Quebec's autonomy. An appeal by Coffin's team to the Cabinet in Ottawa was doubly unsuccessful: the Cabinet decided against a new trial and refused to exercise the royal prerogative of mercy. And Duplessis rejected Coffin's plea to be allowed to marry his long-time partner, Marion Petrie.

On February 9, 1956, Coffin's lawyer François Gravel and his spiritual advisor, Reverend Sam Pollard, visited him in his cell to give him the grim news. *The Gazette* reported Gravel as saying, "I told him that he must hang, that commutation of his death sentence had been denied. He took the bad news like a man. He turned to Mr. Pollard and asked: 'Do you think I can still marry Marion?' Mr. Pollard told him that, too, had been refused."

"I am convinced," added Gravel, "that Coffin is innocent."

The following morning, the hanging proceeded.

Was this a case of cynical political opportunism warping the path of justice? Firebrand author, publisher, and future senator Jacques Hébert certainly thought so. He believed that the case was the biggest legal miscarriage in the history of Quebec, and he published two books to say just that. In the second one, *J'accuse les assassins de Coffin* (I accuse Coffin's assassins), published in 1963, he fingered the Duplessis government for making Coffin the fall guy in the hunters' murder in order to protect the province's lucrative tourist industry. This sparked a royal commission in 1964 to investigate the affair. The commission concluded that Coffin had received a fair trial.

When the bell tolled seven times and the black flag was raised at Montreal's Bordeaux jail on Friday, February 10, 1956, signalling the death of Wilbert Coffin, it did not mark the end of the story. The long-simmering debate on how to deal with the possibility of miscarriage of justice in Canada was heating up. The boiling point would be reached through a case that began in Clinton, Ontario, on a sunny June afternoon in 1959, with the thermometer hovering at the thirty-one-degree-Celsius mark. It was a case that would take nearly fifty years to shuffle along to its imperfect end.

CHAPTER 12

Steven Murray Truscott:
A Kid on Death Row

Tuesday evening, June 9, 1959. Steven Truscott, a popular, athletic fourteen-year-old schoolboy is riding his bike with his buddies on a bridge just outside the town of Clinton, Ontario.

Early Saturday morning, June 13, 1959. Steven Truscott is in prison, accused of the rape and murder of a twelve-year-old classmate.

What happened?

After an early dinner on that hot and steamy Tuesday, Lynne Harper left her house on the Royal Canadian Air Force base around 5:00 p.m. She was headed for the school to help organize a Brownie meeting. When she hadn't returned home by 11:20 p.m., her worried father reported her missing to the air force police. The following morning, with his daughter still nowhere to be found, Leslie Harper knocked on his neighbours' doors to ask if anyone had seen her the night before.

Yes, said Steven Truscott. At around 7:30 p.m., Lynne had asked him to give her a ride on his bike to Highway 8. She told him that she was mad at her parents because they wouldn't take her swimming, and she was planning to hitch a ride to see some ponies. With Lynne sitting on the crossbar of his bike, Steven pedalled along County Road, which led north from the school and over a bridge to the highway. After dropping her off, Steven headed back toward town to join his friends. At the bridge, he turned and looked back. He saw Lynne climb into a grey Chevy with yellow stickers or licence plates. That was the last time he saw her.

Had she run away? No. Two days later, her half-nude body was found covered with branches near Lawson's Bush, a wooded area situated to the east of County Road just before the bridge. Her clothes were neatly folded beside her — other than her blouse, which had been used to strangle her.

By that time, the police had already questioned Steven a few times, on occasion pulling him out of class to do so. They had also decided that they had their man, or rather, their boy. And in the very early morning of June 13, the boy was formally charged with the murder of Cheryl Lynne Harper and taken into custody.

Two police officers accompany Steven Truscott to the Huron County courthouse after his arrest for murdering a schoolmate in 1959. He was fourteen years old at the time.

Steven was only fourteen years old, but a juvenile court magistrate decided that he should be tried as an adult before a judge and jury. This meant that in spite of his age, he could be sentenced to death if found guilty of murder. Steven pleaded not guilty at his trial in Goderich, Ontario.

Crown prosecutor Glenn Hays's case against Steven leaned heavily on the medical evidence, which was damning. District pathologist Dr. John L. Penistan had performed the autopsy on Lynne's body. Basing his opinion on an examination of the contents of Lynne's stomach, he testified that the time of death was between 7:15 and 7:45 p.m. on June 9. Doctors John Addison and David Brooks added their expert testimony to Penistan's. Two sores found on Steven's penis during a physical exam shortly after Lynne's death were believed to have been caused by the sexual assault on the girl; in Brooks's words: "A very inexpert attempt at penetration."

Eyewitnesses testified that Steven was with Lynne during that period, which Steven himself had admitted. No one else was seen with her that evening. Testimony from two of Steven's classmates helped to incriminate him further. Jocelyne Gaudet claimed that Steven had invited her to look for calves that evening near Lawson's Bush, where Lynne's body was found (implication: for sex), but their plans fell through. Another classmate, Butch George, said that Steven had told him that he and Lynne had been near the bush on the night of the murder. Hays skilfully explained away the fact that both these kids had changed their stories since their first statements to the police.

There was no clear evidence, said Hays, that Steven and Lynne had actually crossed the bridge and gone as far as Highway 8. They must have turned off into the woods before reaching the bridge. And that's where Steven killed Lynne.

As for defence attorney Frank Donnelly — well, years later, Truscott told journalist Bill Trent that he distrusted the man from the very beginning. But it is fair to say that Donnelly was hamstrung by a lack of resources and limited access to police and prosecution files.

Donnelly called witness Dr. Berkely Brown, an expert on both the digestive system and rape cases. Brown argued that using the contents of the stomach to establish the time of death was unreliable, as food can remain undigested in the stomach for longer than four hours after a meal.

The lesions on Steven's penis, he said, were most likely not caused by sexual intercourse. Steven had told doctors Addison and Brooks that he had had the lesions for a few weeks, but this was not admitted as evidence. It was later shown that they were caused by a dermatological condition.

Donnelly tried to demonstrate that Steven had met Lynne in the schoolyard well after 7:00 p.m. Steven would not have had time to murder Lynne and rush back to the bridge within the narrow thirty-minute time-of-death window suggested by Penistan.

As an antidote to Gaudet and George, classmates Dougie Oates and Gordon Logan testified on Steven's behalf. They claimed that they saw Steven dropping Lynne off at Highway 8 and returning alone across the bridge to join his pals. According to them, Steven was nowhere near Lawson's Bush around 7:45 that evening. Also, people who met and spoke with Steven that evening described his behaviour as completely normal.

In his summing-up, Justice Robert Ferguson said that no one saw Steven kill Lynne, which meant that all the evidence was circumstantial. The jury, then, should be sure that the circumstances were all consistent with Steven's guilt, and inconsistent with any other reasonable explanation.

The judge was not impressed with Steven's friends Oates and Logan, or their versions of the events clearly supporting Steven's story that he had left Lynne at Highway 8. Their evidence was shaky, said the judge, and there was no direct proof that Steven and Lynne had crossed the bridge.

The jury of twelve was all male. (Defence lawyer Donnelly told Steven's mother, Doris, that although women jurors were permissible by 1959, they were a bad option for this case as they would have been too emotional.) It took them less than four hours to deliver their verdict: guilty, with a plea for mercy.

On Wednesday evening, September 30, 1959, Judge Ferguson ignored the jury's request and Steven received the automatic sentence — death by hanging. His execution was set for December 8, 1959.

Steven was taken back to his small cell at the Huron County Gaol in Goderich, which had now become the death row cell of a convicted murderer. The rules had changed. He was no longer permitted to exercise in the prison yard or join other prisoners for meals. His only outing was to take a shower once a week.

Initially, he wept. "At night time you lie there and cry," he told Julian Sher, author of *Until You Are Dead*. "But it doesn't really accomplish that much. So after a while you even stop doing that. You kind of harden yourself up for what's to come."

But the dread remained. "I woke up one day and somebody was building something outside the wall. You could hear the hammering. I figured they were building scaffolding [for the gallows]. It's just kind of living in terror because nobody tells you any different and it's getting closer and closer to the date that they set."

You would have to go back to 1875 to find a boy as young as Steven languishing for months on death row in Canada. A fourteen-year-old First Nations youth, Quanamcan, was tried, convicted, and sentenced to death for the murder of a mother and her son in Nanaimo, British Columbia. After a recommendation for mercy from the jury, his sentence was commuted to ten years' imprisonment. The last teenager actually executed was Archie McLean, sixteen, youngest member of the Kamloops Outlaws that terrorized the Fort Kamloops area of British Columbia in the late 1870s. He and his fellow gang members were hanged in January 1881.

Would Steven Truscott, seventy-eight years later, also face the gallows?

Steven's lawyers appealed his conviction, first to the Ontario Court of Appeal. This was dismissed. An application for leave to appeal to the Supreme Court of Canada was denied. There was no way, however, that Prime Minister John Diefenbaker was going to sanction the hanging of a fourteen-year-old. By that time, changes to the Criminal Code were being considered, especially with regard to juvenile offenders; in 1956, for example, a special joint committee of the House and Senate had recommended removing the death penalty for children younger than eighteen. In January 1960, the Cabinet stepped in and commuted Steven's death sentence to life imprisonment.

Steven Truscott: bounced from death row at the Huron County Gaol in Goderich to the Ontario Training School for Boys in Guelph, and, when he turned eighteen, to the Collins Bay Penitentiary in Kingston. What was a boy to do? What *this* boy did was train in the machine and carpentry shops and participate in sports programs. In 1969, after ten years in prison, he was eligible for parole. A perfect record meant that he had no problem gaining his release at the age of twenty-four. He changed his name and moved to Guelph, where he married, had three children, and worked as a millwright.

But while Steven Truscott got on with his own quiet, dignified life in the shadows, the case itself obstinately refused to fade into the sepia foot-notes of history. Lawyers, writers, and a gutsy new breed of investigative journalists began to make a difference.

A moving poem in the *Toronto Star* by Canadian historian, author, and journalist Pierre Berton, called "Requiem for a Fourteen-Year-Old," started the ball rolling six days after Truscott was sentenced to death. Berton lambasted the way the criminal justice system had treated the "small, scared boy" in Goderich, a boy who would probably be reprieved ("We always do"), then put in prison to rot. Berton received a deluge of hate mail for his pains. How dare he defend a convicted killer, his critics exclaimed. His own daughter should be raped by a sex fiend, too, they said.

One person who did not hate Berton and his poem was Toronto writer and social activist Isabel LeBourdais, whose own son, coincident-ally, was fourteen years old at the time. LeBourdais started digging and then wrote a book called *The Trial of Steven Truscott*. The book dropped like a stick of dynamite onto the desks of Canadian publishers. Not one of them would touch it and risk a costly court battle. It was eventually published in Britain in 1966, and only then picked up by Canadian com-pany McClelland & Stewart.

"Who killed Lynne Harper?" LeBourdais asks in her final chapter. "Some man with a very sick mind raped and strangled the young girl that night.… They said Steven had done it.… Every witness, every clue, every fact that did not support a case against him was overlooked or ignored from the hour the body of Lynne was found. *Why?*"

The media continued to keep awareness of the Truscott case in the public eye — but an on-camera tear from the eye of Laurier LaPierre after an interview with Doris Truscott for the CBC's *This Hour Has Seven Days* led to both his firing (as it indicated possible bias in his reporting) and the canning of the show in 1966.

In the 1970s, author Bill Trent published two books about Truscott. Then, in the late 1990s, the CBC brought its sizable resources into the fray. The result was a *Fifth Estate* documentary called "Steven Truscott: His Word Against History," produced by Julian Sher and hosted by Linden MacIntyre, which aired in March 2000.

Who killed Lynne Harper? The documentary came up with one highly possible answer to Isabel LeBourdais's anguished question. It described a long-lost psychiatric file — that of Sergeant Alexander Kalichuk, an airman stationed in Clinton in the late 1950s with a "weakness for alcohol and little girls." In spite of a history of sexual offences, and in spite of police warnings to the public, Kalichuk was never considered a suspect. He died of alcoholism in 1975.

In 2001, the Association in Defence of the Wrongly Convicted (now Innocence Canada) launched an application for ministerial review of Steven's conviction under what was then Section 690 of the Criminal Code. The wheels were turning faster now, with public opinion firmly on Steven's side.

In June 2006, the Ontario Court of Appeal conducted a three-week hearing where fresh evidence was heard.

If you had been sitting in the jury box at Steven's trial back in 1959, would you have gone with district pathologist John Penistan's expert opinion on Lynne's time of death, or that of internal medicine specialist Berkely Brown? If you said John Penistan — bad choice. Because as early as 1966, even Dr. Penistan had rejected Dr. Penistan's expert opinion in what he called an "agonizing reappraisal" of his autopsy findings. As it emerged at the hearing in 2006, the good doctor had tried out at least two other time-of-death scenarios before settling on the thirty-minute window: the first version had Lynne's death occurring some time after midnight on June 10; the second put the time of death as much later on the morning of June 10. Both these versions would have exonerated Steven, who had an alibi for those times. Neither was made available to the defence or jurors during Steven's trial.

Given Penistan's flip-flopping about the time of Lynne's death, the Court of Appeal concluded that the doctor's evidence was "reasonably open to the allegation that his opinion shifted to coincide with the Crown's case."

The court also declared that Steven's conviction had been a miscarriage of justice that "must be quashed." And what did that mean, you may ask? It meant that egregious errors of procedure or law had occurred, serious enough for his conviction to be overturned.

Steven had not proved "his factual innocence" — vital DNA evidence that might have identified the killer was lost, presumed destroyed — but in August 2007, the Ontario Court of Appeal finally acquitted him of the murder, meaning that his guilt could not be proven beyond a reasonable doubt.

The Ontario government, through their spokesman Attorney General Michael Bryant, was quick to issue an apology (always much easier to do when an individual has not already been hanged): "The court has found in this case, in light of fresh evidence, that a miscarriage of justice has occurred. And for that miscarriage of justice, on behalf of the government, I am truly sorry."

The last words, though, belong to Steven Truscott. He maintained his innocence from the very beginning, and his story never changed, even though it took forty-eight years for him to clear his name. As reported in the *Toronto Star* in August 2007, he said, "They finally got it right after all these years. I'm so used to fighting. Now we don't have to fight anymore."

Steven Truscott received a settlement of $6.5 million from the Ontario government for his pains. His personal battle was over, and he once again retired to the shadows. But he would step back into the fray, he has said, if any attempt were ever again made to reinstate capital punishment in Canada.

CHAPTER 13

The Last Women to Hang

On the morning of Friday, September 9, 1949, Canadian Pacific (CP) Airlines Flight 108, en route from Montreal to Baie-Comeau on Quebec's north coast, made a brief stopover in Quebec City to take on passengers and additional cargo. The baggage was loaded into the freight compartment at the forward left side of the Douglas DC-3. One of the items was a cardboard box labelled FRAGILE, addressed to Alfred Plouffe of Baie-Comeau, which had been delivered as expedited mail just prior to takeoff. The plane was scheduled to resume its flight at 10:20 a.m., but it left five minutes late.

At 10:45 a.m., the plane dropped out of the sky and crashed into a rocky bluff near Sault-au-Cochon, forty miles northeast of Quebec City, before plummeting into dense bush below. Eyewitnesses on the ground agreed that the aircraft had been flying normally when white smoke started billowing from the left side. The plane was still in the air when they heard a deafening blast, which sounded like dynamite exploding. They saw no accompanying fire or flame.

There were nineteen passengers on board — ten men, six women, and three children. All of them were killed, as was the crew of four. Twenty-three people in all perished that morning. Oscar Tremblay, a Canadian National Railways employee working near the crash site, told the *Schenectady Gazette* that "they all died outright. There were arms and legs and even heads torn from bodies.... The front of the plane seemed to be in one piece and it was jammed with broken and twisted bodies as if they had been thrown forward in the crash."

News of the disaster spread like wildfire. Three of the doomed passengers were top New York–based executives of the Kennecott Copper Corporation. With the Cold War heating up, could this be an anti-American attack by Soviet-bloc terrorists?

Forensic investigations confirmed that the crash was no accident. Engineers concluded that the plane disintegrated in mid-air on account of an explosion caused by what they called "an exterior agent" placed in the left front luggage compartment. Traces of explosives were found among the debris. It turned out that the plane had been brought down by a time bomb stuffed with dynamite and triggered by an electric fuse, a battery, and a clock mechanism.

Fears of a Communist plot were soon dispelled. What emerged instead was a sordid tale of adultery and murder. As Quebec appeal court judge Bernard Bissonnette put it: "It clearly appear[ed] that the principal characters of this pathetic tragedy constituted a regular sink of moral depravity."

The first of these principal characters was identified within ten days of the blast: Marguerite Ruest Pitre, a thirty-nine-year-old Quebec City waitress. The RCMP described her as the woman in black who had delivered the express package to l'Ancienne-Lorette Airport just before the plane took off from Quebec City. When questioned by the police, Pitre explained that she had dropped off what she thought was a statue at the request of her good friend Joseph Albert Guay. Guay immediately became the main focus of police investigations. The third person implicated in the case was Pitre's brother, clockmaker Généreux Ruest.

Two weeks after the blast, Guay was arrested and charged with murder. Police claimed that he had masterminded the bombing with the express purpose of killing his wife, who had been a passenger on the downed aircraft.

Thirty-year-old Guay was described by newspapers of the day as "a slim, wavy-haired Quebec jeweller," "boyish looking," and "dapper." A year earlier, he had fallen firmly and acrimoniously out of love with his wife and the mother of his child, Rita Morel, and madly in love with a seventeen-year-old waitress, Marie-Ange Robitaille. Guay was a close friend of Pitre's and the employer of her brother Généreux Ruest. Guay could always count on Pitre's enthusiastic support. After Robitaille's parents kicked her out, disgusted by her illicit relationship with a married man, Pitre took her in. When Robitaille broke off her liaison with Guay, it was Pitre who persuaded her to kiss and make up. What might have contributed to Pitre's great intimacy with Guay was that the jeweller had given financial assistance to her and her husband, Arthur Pitre, with loans of up to $1,500. In August 1949, the couple still owed him about $600 on two promissory notes, which Guay had finally handed over to his bank for collection.

Guay himself was deeply in debt. With his business failing and his love life falling apart, he opted for the easy way out. He would simply purchase a life insurance policy on his wife … and then get rid of her. What better way to collect a tidy sum of money, save his business from bankruptcy, and marry his mistress?

In August 1949, according to Robitaille, Pitre had told her that Guay intended to poison his wife. But he soon came up with a darker plan. He asked Pitre to purchase ten pounds of dynamite, which she dutifully obtained from a hardware store in Quebec City. That evening she handed Guay the twenty sticks of explosives along with dynamite caps and fuses. Guay's initial idea was to pay a taxi-driver friend, Roland Beaulieu, to take Morel for a ride, during which Beaulieu would jump from the car. The dynamite secreted in the trunk would explode, and Morel would be blown to smithereens. Beaulieu refused point-blank.

Guay's final scheme was conceived in late August and executed in September 1949. He enlisted the help of Ruest, generally described in the press as "a crippled watch-maker," to manufacture a dynamite-detonating device. According to Ruest, Guay had told him that the purpose of the bomb was to clear land he owned at Sept-Îles, Quebec. Guay persuaded his wife to fly to Sept-Îles on a buying trip on September 9 and told Pitre to air-freight the package containing the time bomb on the same plane.

From then on, it would be smooth sailing. The bomb was set to go off when the DC-3 would be flying over the St. Lawrence River, and it would plunge into the water and, presumably, disappear with little prospect of a proper investigation. But the best-laid plans often go astray, let alone the poorly conceived ones. The plane left a few minutes late, as planes often do, and the bomb detonated over land — which greatly simplified the search for answers.

For Pitre, the fallout from the bombing was swift. She tried (unsuccessfully) to commit suicide, claiming that Guay had urged her to do so about ten days after the crash. He even supplied her with "little white pills" to speed things along. At that time, she said, he shocked her with the information that the package she delivered to the airport had contained a bomb, and she would be held responsible for the murders.

Guay's case went to trial in February 1950. Crown prosecutor Noel Dorion called Lucille Levesque to the witness box. She was the CP Air employee who had sold Guay a ticket for the doomed flight. Guay, the *Montreal Gazette* reported, paid $40.40 for his wife's return ticket to Sept-Îles. As for his wife's life, fifty cents was what he obviously considered it was worth — that's what he paid for the $10,000 life insurance policy he bought at the same time. On cross-examination, Levesque stated that she had not tried to sell Guay insurance; he had specifically asked for it. A few hours after the crash, Guay showed up at her counter with his little daughter in tow. He burst into tears and had to be consoled by a priest when told that the plane had been downed with no survivors.

Dorion called Guay "a hypocrite with a diabolical turn of mind." On March 14, 1950, Judge Albert Sévigny openly wept as he gave his charge to the twelve-man French-speaking jury. "The law of God and of her country gave Mrs. Albert Guay the right to live. Nothing escapes the law of God. You have to fulfill the law of your country."

The jury took just seventeen minutes to carry out this duty. They returned a verdict of guilty.

Ruest and Pitre both swore their innocence, but Guay had no intention of going down alone. In a damning statement after his conviction, he confessed to the crime and fingered the sister-and-brother pair as his accomplices.

Guay was hanged at Montreal's Bordeaux jail on January 12, 1951, for the murder of twenty-three people. Reportedly, his last words were "Bien, au moins je meurs célèbre!" ("Well, at least I die famous!").

Ruest was arrested on June 6, 1950, and tried in November of that year.

In his earlier testimony as a Crown witness at Guay's trial, Ruest freely admitted that he had manufactured the detonator for the bomb, but he insisted that the work had been done on Guay's instructions. He also claimed that he had no knowledge of the real purpose of the device. He was clearly terrified of his boss. As reported in the *Montreal Gazette*, before being arrested, Guay had said to him: "You'd better watch out. If you say anything to the police about the work you did for me you'll have me to deal with."

Much of the evidence against Ruest was circumstantial, and many have questioned whether he actually was a party to the plot. But he, too, was sentenced to death by hanging. Suffering from crippling osseous tuberculosis, he was transported to the gallows in a wheelchair. He died, aged fifty-four, on July 25, 1952.

Marguerite Pitre — or Madame le Corbeau (Mrs. Crow), as the press called her because she always wore black — was arrested on June 14, 1950, and her trial began on March 6, 1951. The Crown claimed that her motive for murder was purely financial: Guay had promised to tear up the $600 promissory notes if she ferried the time bomb to the airport.

As pointed out by Greenwood and Boissery, a mountain of circumstantial evidence tipped the scales against Pitre. She had very close and personal ties to Guay, acting as go-between in his amorous activities. Her brother had worked for the jeweller, and the three of them had been spotted talking behind closed doors just before the bombing. She had known in August that Guay wanted to dispose of his wife. And the most damning question of all: exactly when did she learn that the package contained a bomb? She contended it was ten days after the blast, but her own husband testified that she had told him at the time of delivery that the parcel was dangerous.

The French-speaking, twelve-man jury deliberated for twenty-nine minutes. Guilty. Trial judge Noel Belleau was harsh: "It is not necessary for me to add that with such an odious crime, of which the accused has been found guilty, I find it impossible to recommend clemency."

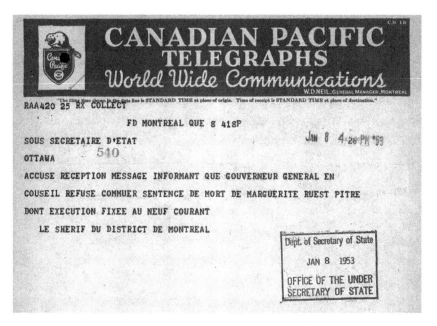

A telegram dated January 8, 1953, conveying the refusal of the Governor-General-in-Council to commute the sentence of Marguerite Pitre. She was hanged the following day, making her the last woman ever executed in Canada.

By the time Pitre's turn came to meet the hangman, both Guay and Ruest had been hanged, and her husband, Arthur, had died after a short illness.

On January 9, 1953, beneath the headline "Buxom Widow Pitre Goes To Gallows For Part In Time-Bombing Of Plane," the *Ottawa Citizen* described the last few hours of Marguerite Ruest Pitre's life on earth. On the afternoon of January 8, Pitre was accompanied from Quebec City to the Fullum Street Women's Prison in Montreal by two plainclothes police officers and a nun. The "stocky" Madame le Corbeau was a thinner and much less confident woman than the one who had "punctuated with wisecracks" the murder trials of Guay, her friend-creditor, and Ruest, her brother. She was an angrier one, too. When photographed through the car window, she yelled at policemen that she had been promised no pictures. She was hanged at Bordeaux jail, dropping through the trap at 12:35 a.m., and was pronounced dead at 12:50 a.m.

The details of this case — the air disaster, the loss of twenty-three lives, the sordid actions of those convicted for the murders — made it notable. It was additionally newsworthy because women were so rarely hanged in Canada. The *Ottawa Citizen* noted that Pitre was the first woman to be executed in Quebec since February 1940, when Marie-Louise Cloutier was hanged for murdering her husband, and the first in Canada since Elizabeth Popovitch followed her husband to the scaffold at Welland, Ontario, in December 1946 for the murder of a Thorold shopkeeper.

Of the three, Cloutier was definitely the odd woman out — the only one tried, convicted, and hanged for killing her spouse — although in the grand scheme of things, of the eleven women executed in the period from 1867 to 1976, seven were husband killers. Cloutier was the last of them.

In a place and time — Quebec in the mid-1900s — where the gold standard for womanly behaviour was still the role of wife and mother, Cloutier stood out. She had no children, and after twenty years of marriage to Vilmont Brochu in St-Méthode, Quebec, she was looking for something to spice up life on the farm. In 1936, as noted by Dale Brawn in *Practically Perfect*, she started a relationship with the hired help, Achille Grondin, but conducted another affair on the side with neighbouring farmer Adolphe Gilbert. Both men were besotted, and quite happy to help when she professed the desire to rid herself of her spouse. The two of them hoped to accomplish this by putting a curse on Brochu. Cloutier, very practical, believed that poison would do the job more effectively, and in late 1936, she set to work dosing her husband with arsenic. The months dragged on, but Brochu, despite several bouts of acute illness, stubbornly refused to die. The plotters upped the ante: a two-pronged attack — hex *and* poison — did the trick. Brochu became violently sick and died in August 1937.

By the following day, Cloutier had made a request to have her husband's life insurance policy paid out to her; two days later, Grondin had moved in; and by October, they were married — too speedy by far. Neighbours started whispering, and Brochu's grieving sister took her suspicions to the police. Brochu's body was exhumed, and traces of arsenic indicated that he had not died of indigestion, as stated on his death certificate. The newlyweds were taken into custody during their honeymoon.

Cloutier, dressed in deep mourning black, was tried in September 1938 at St-Joseph-de-Beauce, Quebec.

As criminologist Sylvie Frigon points out, childlessness was seen as central to Cloutier's crime. In his address to the jury, trial judge Noel Belleau (the same judge who would later preside over Pitre's trial) asked: "What could a woman with no children and no tenure in a home do?... When there are no children, a woman alone in a house may be victim to many errors."

After a trial lasting seventeen days, the jury took one hour and fifteen minutes to come to the conclusion that Cloutier's errors had been of the murderous kind, and they returned a verdict of guilty.

Grondin, too, was sentenced to death, and the couple's appeals to the Quebec Court of Appeal and the Supreme Court of Canada all failed. After nearly a year and a half on death row, both were hanged. Although by law the executions should have taken place in the village of St-Joseph-de-Beauce, the locals were horrified at the very thought. They petitioned the Quebec government to move the location to the Bordeaux jail in Montreal. This was granted, and first Grondin then Cloutier walked to the scaffold in the early morning of February 23, 1940.

Like Cloutier and Pitre, thirty-eight-year-old Elizabeth Popovitch was wearing black when she climbed the thirteen steps to the gallows at the Welland County Gaol at 1:00 a.m. on December 5, 1946. Her husband, George, a forty-five-year-old paper maker, had preceded her by forty-five minutes. Both were accompanied on their last journey by the Reverend Harvey G. Forster, the man who had married them one year earlier.

The couple had been tried and convicted of murdering Elizabeth's employer Louis Nato, the owner of a small store in Thorold. In a dying statement at the Maplehurst hospital, reported in the *Niagara Falls Gazette* in August 1946, Nato said that he had been driving the Popovitches in his car when they attacked him. "His money was removed and he was stripped of his trousers. One of his assailants said there was only $280 and there should be more," the hospital's superintendent testified in court. "They then ... began kicking and pounding him. Nato begged for mercy, saying, 'You've got my money, what more do you want?'" Police said that Nato had given Elizabeth $1,000 after her first husband died to pay off her bills and buy clothes for her three children.

Standing among the hundred-strong crowd in the street outside the jail yard, where blazing floodlights had turned night to day for the hanging, were two of Elizabeth's daughters. One of them, just thirteen years old, had visited her in her cell the previous day. The third daughter, reported Gwyn Thomas of the *Toronto Daily Star*, had been "unable to stand the strain" and had fled to the United States a few days earlier. Also present was Elizabeth's distraught brother, who had come from Hamilton hoping to say a last farewell. The bus was delayed, and he missed the 10:00 p.m. cut-off time.

"I asked to see the sheriff," said the man, who wished to remain anonymous to shield his family and job in Hamilton, "and they told me he wouldn't see anybody. I tried everything to see Liz before they hanged her but nobody would see me. Mr. Forster tried to get me in but he had no success. There were ten in our family, but there is one less now."

"God bless him," was the message Popovitch relayed via Forster to her brother, and he broke down in tears.

On January 19, 1649, a young girl of fifteen or sixteen was found guilty of theft and hanged in the town of Quebec. This was purported to be the first execution in Canada. Three hundred years later, also in Quebec, the Sault-au-Cochon air disaster would mark the end of the long-standing Canadian tradition of hanging women.

What irony that the first attack against civil aviation in North America was no terrorist incursion, as originally feared, but a squalid domestic murder. In the mid-1900s, getting a divorce in straitlaced Catholic Quebec was still not a straightforward matter. Would the outcome have been different if Albert Guay had simply been able to separate from his wife? Remembering appeal court judge Bissonnette's view that most of the individuals involved in the tragedy were "a regular sink of moral depravity," and his further comments that they lacked "personal decency and the most elementary rules of moral conduct," it would probably not have made the slightest difference to Guay's decision to bring down a plane to kill Rita Morel, without concern for the other innocent victims who would surely perish with her.

And what of Ruest and Pitre, who were originally viewed as dupes but subsequently tried and convicted as Guay's accomplices? The evidence against Ruest was mostly circumstantial, and he was very possibly not guilty. Pitre's situation was more complicated. Some commentators have suggested that she may have been innocent, a position held by two of her judges of appeal. Pitre loudly protested her innocence to the end, but her tight and cozy relationship with Guay sank her.

Marguerite Pitre stepped onto the scaffold in the early morning of January 9, 1953. Afterwards, prison authorities said that she showed no fear and that "everything was normal." This brought the tally of women hanged in Quebec since Confederation to five. And she was the eleventh, and last, woman ever executed in Canada.

It would take another nine years to bring to an end the hanging of men.

CHAPTER 14

The Last Drop

Imagine sitting down to question someone wearing a terrifying black mask with slits cut out for eyeholes! That's what happened to CBC reporter Paul Soles in a television interview with Canada's last hangman just before capital punishment was abolished in 1976.

Looking like a deer caught in the headlights, Soles asked John Ellis if he wore the mask for executions.

"No," replied Ellis. "All I wear is a black suit, black bow tie, white shirt, and black shoes. I'm not there to frighten him. I'm there to execute him."

"If the vote goes for abolition," asked Soles, "and there's no longer a need of a hangman, how do you think you personally will feel?"

"Well, I'll feel that I've served the country in the best way that I know how.... I have met the requirements that the country required. I've done my job and I'm retired."

What became of Ellis when the vote *did* go for abolition in 1976, putting an abrupt end to his professional career? According to one account, the retiree, in his fifties at the time, spent the winter months in Florida like thousands of other Canadian snowbirds; another report in 1984 stated that he was living in the Bahamas.

It is quite surprising that we know so little about Canada's last hangman. John Ellis was not his real name, but one he adopted, like several other executioners before him, in honour of John Ellis, a well-known

British executioner in the early 1900s. Was Ellis a farmer from Ontario, as some have suggested? Or a travelling salesman who went to church regularly? Or was he actually the owner of a trailer park in Ontario, somewhere between Belleville and Kingston?

We don't know what Ellis looked like, either. However, Mark Bonokoski, a *Toronto Sun* reporter who met him face to face in 1975, did shed a little light on the enigmatic Mr. Ellis: "I didn't know exactly what to expect from a hangman, but I certainly wasn't expecting a short (maybe 5-foot-8) stocky and somewhat overweight little man with a greying moustache who looked more like a benign bookkeeper."

We do know that John Ellis hanged at least fifteen men. His last job was a double hanging at Toronto's Don Jail in December 1962. From then on, he performed no further official duties.

It looks as if Ellis had quite a stash of pocket money to spend during his first few years of retirement, though. Tucked into the 1985 annual report of Ontario's provincial auditor (along with a critique of the Liquor Control Board of Ontario for cost overruns and the Ontario Provincial Police for massively overstocking on items such as heavy winter breeches) was the revelation that the Ontario government still had the hangman on its payroll, even though his last working day had been more than twenty years previous. According to a report in the *Toronto Star* in November 1985, Ontario paid a "provincial executioner" $200 a month for eight years after the abolition of capital punishment in 1976, which, according to provincial auditor Douglas Archer, added up to the tidy sum of $20,000.

Brian Pitkin, appointed York County sheriff in 1984, alerted the auditor to the monthly cheques, and the payments were stopped. Pitkin felt it was unlikely that the services of a hangman would ever again be required, even if there were a return to capital punishment in the future. But he had nothing further to add to our meagre cache of information about John Ellis. When interviewed by Bonokoski in 1987, he said: "As a matter of fact, I cannot even remember [Ellis's] real name any more. All I remember is sending him his last retainer cheque, somewhere around October or November in 1984." His final contact was a call to Ellis some time later to see if he was interested in a hanging job in Delaware. Ellis was not.

One thing we know for certain: John Ellis was a firm believer in capital punishment. As he told the CBC's Paul Soles in 1976, "I feel that people are … that has so much to say about capital punishment has never seen an execution. They don't realize just how humane it is." Criminals, he added, preferred it to life imprisonment.

What unfolded in 1962 after the murder trials of the last two prisoners facing execution in Canada stands in stark contrast to Ellis's claim that criminals preferred hanging. Arthur Lucas and Ronald Turpin did not want to die, and appeals to save them began immediately after the death sentence was imposed on them on May 10 and June 13 respectively. There were letter-writing campaigns, television programs, and newspaper articles and editorials. The two men's spiritual advisor at the Don Jail, Salvation Army chaplain Cyril Everitt, sent impassioned pleas to Canada's prime minister and the minister of justice on their behalf, and a team of lawyers championed their cause right up to the Supreme Court of Canada.

All the appeals failed. And so the paths of Ronald Turpin, Arthur Lucas, and John Ellis collided just after midnight on December 11, 1962. While a group of protesters waved banners in the bitter cold outside the Don Jail (CHRISTMAS IN A GRAVE, HANGING IS ALSO MURDER), Turpin and Lucas stood back to back on the gallows platform with black hoods over their heads. The hangman sprang the trap and down they went together, plummeting into history as the last two men hanged in Canada.

As shown by Robert Hoshowsky in *The Last to Die*, Turpin and Lucas came from radically different backgrounds.

Ronald Turpin was born and raised, if you could call it that, in Toronto. Psychiatric assessments at the time of his trial revealed him to be an angry and damaged individual, his childhood poisoned with physical, emotional, and sexual abuse. His mother struggled with her own demons and often found solace in alcohol. When Turpin was eleven, his mother turned him over to the Children's Aid Society. He never forgave her for taking that step, which he regarded as her ultimate act of cruelty. He bounced from foster home to foster home, and once he hit his teens, from reformatory to reformatory. Before he entered adulthood, his litany of convictions already included shoplifting, burglary, car theft, forgery, and escaping from custody. Along with his criminal record, he carried a fear of police bordering on paranoid. He told everyone who would listen that the cops were out to get him.

So when he broke into the Red Rooster Restaurant in Scarborough to steal $632.84 in bills and coins in the frigid early morning hours of February 12, 1962, Turpin, twenty-nine years old, was already very well known to Toronto police. As he drove away after the robbery in his rusty old Pontiac truck with bald tires and a battered right front headlight taped into position, he met his nemesis — a Toronto police officer in his cruiser. Constable Frederick John Nash, a thirty-one-year-old married man with four kids, had just come on duty, and he pulled the truck over. Nash hauled Turpin out of the vehicle and grabbed the keys. Unfortunately, along with his loot, Turpin had a loaded Beretta semi-automatic pistol stashed under his seat — and Nash found the gun.

There were no witnesses to what happened next. By the time passers-by and other officers came on the scene, Nash lay dying on the roadway, his body peppered with bullets; Turpin was wounded in his arms and face.

"He shot me first" was one of the last things Nash said. Turpin, however, insisted that Nash attacked him first, slamming him against the police car, and was pistol-whipping him when the gun went off in Turpin's face.

The bottom line was that Turpin had killed a policeman. And without remorse, it seemed. "Everybody's gotta go sometime," he said with a shrug, as reported later by homicide detective Jim Crawford. Turpin was charged with murder.

The stakes were high. By 1961, the law had been changed to differentiate between capital murder, which carried the death sentence, and non-capital murder, which would result in a life sentence. Killing a cop was a capital offence.

Arthur Lucas, who died on the scaffold with Turpin, was an African-American gangster born in Cordele, Georgia, in 1907. According to some reports, Lucas arrived in Toronto in November 1961 with murder on his mind. His mission, they said, was to execute Therland Crater, a police informant from Detroit who was scheduled to give evidence in an upcoming drug trial, and his girlfriend, Carolyn Ann Newman, who worked as a prostitute.

DROP DEAD

November 17, 1961. The grim sequence of events began at 6:30 a.m. on that chilly fall morning with a terrified call to a Bell telephone operator. As the call progressed, the horror-struck operator, Elizabeth Williams, heard "a series of really loud screams and then a few moments later there was like a fumbling sound, like as if somebody was perhaps trying to get the receiver, and a kind of like baby cries." Realizing that she was plugged in to the gruesome sounds of a woman being murdered, she put the call through to the police emergency operator. When the police arrived at the rooming house in the quiet Annex suburb where this scene had played out, they found the two victims. Their throats had been slashed with gangland efficiency. Crater had also been shot four times, perhaps to make sure that he was truly dead.

"Double Murder Victims Executed By Hired Killers," howled the Toronto newspapers. The hunt was on to purge Toronto of this spate of American gangsters infecting the city with theft, drugs, and prostitution.

Lucas soon became a person of police interest. He lived in Detroit, where he had a history of drug dealings with Crater. He was in Toronto at the time of the murders and had visited Crater and Newman earlier that very morning. There were bloodstains in his car. He owned a .38 Iver Johnson revolver, the type used to shoot Crater. The gun was subsequently found by a safety patrol officer on the Burlington Skyway bridge, located on one of the main routes between Toronto and Detroit. He owned the heavy gold ring that was found on the bloodstained bed inches away from Newman's dead body. Lucas was arrested in Detroit twenty-one hours after the slayings and extradited to Canada, where he was tried for the murder of Crater.

His mug shot shows a heavy-set, sullen man with close-cropped black hair and large, bulgy, expressionless eyes. A slew of psychiatric reports described him as anti-social, vicious, and, with an IQ of 63, having the intellect of a "moron." What he shared with Turpin was a history of childhood abandonment and abuse and an extensive criminal record. His crimes — forgery, armed robbery, drug trafficking, and pimping — were much more serious than Turpin's, and much more violent.

The trial of *Regina v. Lucas* began in Toronto on April 30, 1962. Before long, as noted by Hoshowsky, the Crown had built up a strong

Arthur Lucas at the time of his arrest in 1961. Doubt persists to this day as to whether Lucas was capable of planning and executing a double murder with the precision of a professional hit man.

but largely circumstantial case, so circumstantial that Ross MacKay, the lawyer defending Lucas, complained bitterly to the judge.

"The difficulty is, Mr. MacKay, that you do not regard circumstantial evidence as a matter of each piece being consistent with innocence," replied the judge. "The question for the jury to decide is on the collective circumstances, are they consistent with innocence." Does this sound familiar? Justice James Chalmers McRuer was the same judge who had stressed the admissibility of circumstantial evidence in the Sullivan manslaughter case some eleven years previous.

MacKay was everyone's dream lawyer: young (twenty-nine years old), charismatic, drop-dead gorgeous, and fast gaining a reputation as a top-notch criminal lawyer. However, in spite of his charm and multiple talents, he did not find a sympathetic ear with McRuer.

The veteran judge was then in his seventies. He was regarded as a great legal reformer at the time (and still is). In addition, he had presided at multiple murder trials, sending many convicted murderers to the gallows, including Boyd Gang members Steve Suchan and Lennie Jackson in 1952. For this, he had earned the nickname "Hanging Jim." His other nickname was "Vinegar Jim," and MacKay, to his dismay, saw much of this side of McRuer's character during the trial. For example, when MacKay objected to having the shocking, bloody pictures of Carolyn Newman taken at the crime scene and at the morgue admitted as evidence, the judge overruled him.

As shown during the appeal process and in a series of investigative reports in the years that followed, the case against Lucas was seriously flawed. The court relied on damning testimony from Lucas's friend, drug addict and drug dealer Morris "Red" Thomas, who claimed that Lucas had been run out of Toronto by morality officers. Thomas also identified both the gold ring found at the crime scene and the gun found on the Burlington Skyway as belonging to Lucas. However, the gun was not positively identified by ballistics experts as the weapon that fired the bullets into Crater's body. Other troubling questions persist. Why was no real effort made to locate Willie White, who shared Lucas's hotel room in Toronto and who might have provided him with an alibi? How could such a slow-witted, slow-moving individual as Lucas have planned and executed a double murder with the precision of a professional hit man? Lucas's fingerprints were all over his car; why were none of his prints found at the crime scene?

In his summing up for the defence at the trial, Ross MacKay tried his best to raise some doubts of his own to prove that Lucas didn't "fit the bill." Given the amount of blood that spurted out at the murder scene, why weren't Lucas's clothes drenched with blood if he had done the killing? If he were a professional killer, why would he register at a hotel using his own name? And would a hit man pay social visits to his victims before killing them, as Lucas openly claimed to have done? Who could believe the testimony of the drug addict and liar who claimed to be Lucas's friend? And who could prove that the gun found on the Skyway belonged to Lucas?

It was a hopeless task. On May 10, 1962, the all-white, all-male jury came back after five hours with a verdict of guilty.

Then, and right to the end, Lucas continued to proclaim his innocence.

— — —

MacKay found himself in the hot seat again three weeks later, when he returned to court at Toronto's City Hall to defend Ronald Turpin. Again, with few resources and little money, the odds were stacked against him and his client. Judge George Gale allowed the jury to probe Turpin's previous record to establish if he was the kind of person likely to shoot a police officer. MacKay, however, was not permitted to question the good name of Frederick Nash, the police officer who was shot.

MacKay had a fatal flaw: an excessive weakness for alcohol. By that time, he was drinking heavily. Lucas had been aware of this during his trial and was harshly critical. "The lawyer … drank," he complained later. "Well, you could smell it."

During Turpin's exceedingly stressful trial, MacKay's alcohol abuse became more and more noticeable. He would show up late for court, sometimes clearly suffering from the after-effects of a binge. And he was scattered, not focused enough on what might have been Turpin's strongest defence: that he had acted in self-defence.

Again, the jury took just a few short hours to deliver their verdict on June 13, 1962: guilty, with no recommendation for mercy.

Lucas and Turpin spent their final days on death row in the Don Jail talking, reading the Bible, and singing hymns with their spiritual advisor, Cyril Everitt. On the day before they were hanged, they ate their last meal at 6:00 p.m. (steak, potatoes, vegetables, and pie), then received a visit from Lucas's appeal lawyer, Walter Williston. Williston confirmed the grim news — all their appeals had failed. They would be dead before morning.

As reported by Hoshowsky, Williston added, "If it's any consolation to you, you may be the last men to hang in Canada."

"Some consolation," said Turpin.

At midnight, Turpin and Lucas met John Ellis. The hangman would receive $1,000 from the York County sheriff's office for the next few minutes' work.

At 12:01 a.m. on December 11, 1962, with Everitt walking alongside,

EXCLUSIVE CONNECTION WITH WESTERN UNION CABLE SERVICE   Form 6102

CANADIAN NATIONAL TELEGRAPHS
J. R. WHITE GENERAL MANAGER TORONTO

Send the following message, subject to the terms on back hereof, which are hereby agreed to

OTTAWA   DECEMBER 10, 1962.

W. C. BOWMAN, ESQ., Q.C.,
DIRECTOR OF PUBLIC PROSECUTIONS
ATTORNEY GENERAL'S DEPARTMENT
PARLIAMENT BUILDINGS
TORONTO ONTARIO

GOVERNOR GENERAL IN COUNCIL WILL NOT INTERFERE WITH DEATH

SENTENCES PASSED UPON ARTHUR LUCAS CONVICTED FOR THE CAPITAL

MURDER OF THERLAND CRATER AND UPON RONALD TURPIN CONVICTED FOR

THE CAPITAL MURDER OF CONSTABLE NASH.

D H CHRISTIE
DIRECTOR   CRIMINAL LAW SECTION
Charge: Justice Dept.   DEPARTMENT OF JUSTICE
       Legal Br.

Notification dated December 10, 1962, that the Governor-General-in-Council would not interfere with the death sentences passed on Arthur Lucas and Ronald Turpin. The two men were hanged back to back at Toronto's Don Jail the following morning, making them the last to be hanged in Canada.

the two men were led to the execution chamber and hanged together, back to back.

Final hangings; final gruesome bungle.

Turpin died quickly. But, in an interview with the Salvation Army's internal newsletter, Everitt said, "Lucas's head was torn right off. It was hanging just by the sinews of the neck. There was blood all over the floor."

Had Ellis miscalculated Lucas's weight, as Everitt believed? Perhaps he was drunk, as others suggested. Homicide detective Jim Crawford attended the double hanging and spoke afterward with Ellis. The hangman, said Crawford, was completely sober. Ellis himself had a different theory: the near decapitation was caused by the fact that Lucas had syphilis, which had weakened the bones and blood vessels of his neck.

The ultimate irony: one of the last two men hanged in Canada was every hangman's nightmare — a heavy man with a weak neck.

CHAPTER 15

Under Lock and Key

When Arthur Lucas and Ronald Turpin dropped through the trap door in December 1962, a ninety-year-old Toronto tradition came to an abrupt end — hangings at the Don Jail. Starting in 1872, thirty-four men in total were executed there.

Executions were initially carried out in the northeast exercise yard, but in 1905, the gallows were moved indoors to a disused latrine in the east wing. Then, in September 2007, during excavations for the new Bridgepoint Health complex being built beside the old jail, a grisly discovery was made: the remains of fifteen executed men in the exercise yard. Newspapers had long dubbed this area "Murderers' Row" or "Murderers' Graveyard." Now, a professional site investigation proved them correct.

To help identify the bodies, old newspaper reports and other archival sources were used to build up a historical profile of the men executed at the Don, with details like their age, or the clothes they were wearing when they were executed, or the location of their burial in the yard. These profiles were then painstakingly compared to archaeological data (shell buttons, a copper cross, the remains of workboots with felt lining) and biological data (missing teeth, metal tooth fillings, prominent nasal bones) found in the field.

One of the fifteen bodies unearthed in the exercise yard by archaeologist Ron Williamson and his team was that of twenty-year-old John

Traviss of Newmarket, Ontario. In a fit of jealous rage, Traviss had shot a rival for the love of a farmer's daughter. He was the very first person to be executed at the Don in 1872 and the first to be buried in the yard.

Also excavated was the grave of George Bennett, alias Dickson, his skeleton still clad in well-preserved remnants of the black suit he had worn for his hanging in 1880. Bennett was an employee of *The Globe* newspaper in Toronto, sacked for "intemperance," a euphemism for excessive drunkenness on the job. In an altercation in March 1880 with his former boss, the proprietor of the newspaper and Father of Confederation George Brown, Bennett pulled out a gun, and in the ensuing scuffle, discharged it. Brown suffered what *The Globe* called "a severe flesh wound." This escalated into a fatal infection, and he died seven weeks later. Bennett was convicted of murder, hanged, and buried in the jail yard on July 23. The last burial at the Don was that of Edward Stewart, a thirty-three-year-old labourer executed on March 24, 1930, for killing a Gerrard Street butcher during a robbery attempt.

By 1930, the requirement that executed persons be buried where they had been hanged was no longer being strictly enforced. From then onward, there were no further burials at the Don — bodies were generally claimed by family or friends. There were exceptions, though; after Arthur Lucas and Ronald Turpin were hanged, their corpses were immediately whisked away by prison officials to be buried at the Prospect Cemetery in Toronto.

In 1931, the mayor of Toronto remarked that many of the cells at the Don Jail were so narrow a fat horse could not be backed into them. By that time the Don was developing a fearsome reputation. A 1952 enquiry, for example, found that "the cells are very small and have no toilet facilities, necessitating the use of night pails.... Due to overcrowding beds have often to be placed in the corridors, under most unsatisfactory conditions." As reported by the *Montreal Gazette* in 1973, an Ontario Supreme Court grand jury called the Don dehumanizing and a potential fire hazard. "Any person, whether convicted or not, would leave this place demoralized and condemning society." Tuberculosis and other diseases caused by overcrowding were rife.

It had all started off with such great promise.

The idea of the new Toronto Jail was put forward in the mid-1800s, as a replacement for the primitive and exhausted hell holes that had until then housed short-term prisoners — those awaiting trial or with sentences of less than two years. The building would be airy and bathed in natural light. There would be a hospice to care for Toronto's "poor, needy and disabled," and a working farm. And what better place to locate all these splendid structures than on a parcel of land overlooking the beautiful, meandering Don River? After all, as British penal reformer John Howard wrote in 1777, "A county gaol, and indeed every prison, should be built on a spot that is airy, and if possible near a river, or brook. I have commonly found prisons situated near a river, the cleanest and most healthy."

The Auburn prison system, established in the United States in the 1820s, heavily influenced both the architecture of the new jail and the proposed treatment of its inmates. There would be a central administrative building with two wings containing long rows of small cells extending to the east and west. During the day, prisoners would toil together on the prison farm or in communal work areas inside the prison; at night, they would be segregated in individual cells. Strict discipline would be imposed and silence maintained at all times.

British immigrant William Thomas, the hotshot architect who had already designed some of Toronto's finest buildings (such as St. Lawrence Hall), was chosen to draw up the plans in 1852. This grand palace for prisoners would have a central pavilion, an Italianate style facade, and columns embellished with wavy, wormlike lines. Construction began in 1858.

From its very beginnings, however, the project was plagued with problems. Thomas died of diabetes in December 1860, leaving his sons to carry on. Construction was way over budget and massively delayed, not helped by a compromised foundation that had to be rebuilt and a fire that destroyed most of the building just before it was completed. Insurance, naturally, didn't cover the costs of reconstruction.

The highly touted farm and airy, light-filled working areas where inmates would spend their days soon went the way of the dodo, and prisoners ended up spending both their waking and sleeping hours crammed into the poky cells. Small wonder there were numerous escape attempts over the years. These were mostly unsuccessful. In one creative effort, as mentioned in Bridgepoint Health's brochure on the history of the Don Jail, James Bass and Melville Yeomans used kitchen utensils to dig a hole, which they concealed with cardboard and strawberry jam. Security guards, perhaps on the hunt for stolen spoons and jam, soon discovered the hole and put an end to their plan. However, Frank McCullough, a drifter awaiting execution for the murder of a police officer in 1918, managed to saw through the bars of his cell and escape, and in 1951 and 1952, members of the Boyd Gang, a flamboyant four-man group of bank robbers, broke out not once but twice.

The original building was officially shut down in 1977. Its replacement, the adjoining east wing completed in 1958, did nothing to improve the tarnished reputation of Toronto's forbidding prison. This extension, in its turn, was closed in 2013 and then demolished to make way for Bridgepoint, a new rehabilitation and complex care hospital.

Toronto's forbidding Don Jail, as pictured in 1949 or 1950. The first man to be executed there was John Traviss in 1872 and the last two, Ronald Turpin and Arthur Lucas, were hanged simultaneously in 1962.

For Torontonians who may have become too big-headed about how appalling their local lock-up was, a reality check: there were others just as squalid scattered throughout the country.

Definitely *not* on the list was the Kingston Penitentiary, commonly known as the Kingston Pen, the grim stone pile that has dominated the eastern end of Lake Ontario since 1833. A penitentiary is a very different animal from a jail. Historically, a jail was a local or provincial institution, its purpose being to serve as a sort of holding tank for prisoners awaiting trial or with sentences of less than two years. A penitentiary, on the other hand, was and still is run on the federal level, a place that houses prisoners serving long terms to atone for their crimes (think "penance"). One of the most common questions asked by curious visitors who stroll across the road from Kingston Pen to Canada's Penitentiary Museum is: Whereabouts in the penitentiary did hangings take place? And the answer is … nowhere. Because executions were the responsibility of local or provincial authorities, Kingston hangings took place at the Frontenac County Gaol, formerly located behind the Frontenac County Court House but demolished in 1973.

Look no further than the Carleton County Gaol on Nicholas Street in Ottawa, Ontario, for an excellent example of a terrible jail. Designed by architect H.H. Horsey, it was regarded as a "model gaol" when it first opened in 1862, embodying the finest principles of prison reform. Its stellar reputation did not last very long. Some of its "features"? No lighting, no ventilation, no heating, no toilets. Buckets, anyone? Hardened criminals mingled with minor offenders, punishments were unnecessarily brutal, and very little effort was made to rehabilitate prisoners. Once described as "a monstrous relic of an imperfect civilization," it was shuttered in 1972. The jail now operates as a hostel — the paying guests don't seem to mind the rather cramped quarters and the resident ghost, which may be that of Patrick James Whelan. Whelan, you will remember, was convicted for the assassination of Thomas D'Arcy McGee and hanged in 1869. He was the first of three men who walked from the narrow cell on death row to the noose dangling from the permanent gallows at this prison. The other two were William George Seabrooke, executed for the murder of a gas station attendant in 1933, and Eugène Larment in 1946, found guilty of shooting a police detective during a botched robbery.

There were other prisons with permanent gallows dotted around the provinces, like Headingley Gaol in Headingley, Manitoba, or Bordeaux jail in Montreal, Quebec. But you would have had to travel way across Canada to find a jail worse than the Don. It's gone now, demolished in 1992, but for seventy-nine years, the Oakalla Prison in Burnaby, British Columbia, served as a model for what a prison should not be.

It didn't start off that way, of course.

Oakalla was conceived as a new centrally located prison farm to serve the lower British Columbian mainland, replacing the hopelessly inadequate institutions that existed at the time. It would hold around 480 prisoners, either sentenced to terms of less than two years, or awaiting trial or transfer to a federal penitentiary. Like the Don, it would embrace the Auburn system of penology — harsh discipline and hard work for inmates during the day, solitary confinement at night. Also like the Don, there would be hangings.

None of that went down well with the locals.

"Not in My Back Yard!" cried the NIMBYists.

"Nonsense," replied the authorities. This prison would usher in a whole new era of penal reform to the province.

Fine intentions, to be sure. But soon after Oakalla's grand opening in 1912, reality proved to be very different. Inmates complained of the noise and violence, and of rats and other infestations. Overcrowding was always a big problem. By the 1950s, the population of the prison averaged well over six hundred, and in the early 1960s, there were often more than a thousand inmates crammed inside. As reported by the *Vancouver Sun*, provincial judge Cunliffe Bartlett, after spending two days at Oakalla in 1979 at the invitation of corrections officials, described the prison as a "cold, hostile environment.... It is hopelessly outdated, old, patched up and not clean."

It was not a very secure place, either. Earl Andersen describes Oakalla in *Hard Place to Do Time* as "a punishing yet easily escapable institution." The statistics he quotes are startling. Between 1940 and 1990, more than 890 men, women, and young offenders escaped from the prison.

Riots and other incidents became commonplace. In April 1936, the *Montreal Gazette* reported that what the warden called a small group of "agitators" had started a food strike over the lack of variety in their diet. "Too much beef!" they beefed. There was "considerable shouting" but no violence on that occasion.

Things were radically different in October 1952 when around a hundred men rioted, causing what *The Gazette* called "heavy property damage," and leading to calls for an emergency program to correct the "shocking conditions."

There were several women's riots in the 1970s and early 1980s, a violent protest in September 1982, and a rampage in November 1983. On New Year's Day 1988, thirteen prisoners, described as armed and dangerous, embarrassingly escaped from the segregation unit, a concrete bunker located under an unused cow barn. They had been sent there after causing disturbances such as rioting, lighting fires, and attacking prison personnel. They claimed their actions were provoked by the behaviour of guards, who beat up an inmate for talking in church. One of the escapees accused the guards of being drunk and turning fire hoses on prisoners in their cells.

But you would agree that a jail like Oakalla was not always a pleasant place to work in, either.

As reported by the *Toledo Blade* in May 1956, Bruce Larsen, city editor of the *Vancouver Province*, spent a horrendously tense afternoon in the prison barbershop bargaining with three inmates who were holding a prison guard hostage. After five hours, and a promise to print their story in a special edition, the convicts removed the razor they were holding to the man's throat and the pair of shears from his back and released him unharmed. "My legs were a little weak, my throat too dry," was Larsen's understatement at the end of the ordeal.

Cunliffe Bartlett, the provincial judge who had spent two days in lock-up at Oakalla in 1979, remarked: "Your first impression is that a lot of good people are trying hard under terrible circumstances to do the best job they can."

In 1919, Oakalla became Hanging Central in British Columbia. Over the next forty years, forty-four prisoners were executed. The first man hanged, on August 29, 1919, was twenty-year-old Alex "The Skunk" Ignace, a young First Nations man who shot his wife on the Kamloops Reserve. On April 28, 1959, tugboat worker Leo Anthony Mantha was the last prisoner executed for the stabbing death of his lover, Aaron Jenkins. There were also several double hangings at Oakalla, and, in 1936, even a triple hanging.

The gallows at Oakalla garnered dubious fame in April 1937 — two prisoners, Gordon Fawcett and Blackie Campbell, coolly made their get-away by gaining entry into the execution chamber itself, possibly aided and abetted by a staff member. As this room was used for storage when it wasn't being used for hangings, the escapees fashioned ropes from sheets and blankets, sawed through the bars on the window, lowered themselves down to the ground, and scuttled off to freedom. Campbell was shot to death in a botched bank robbery some months later. Fawcett, who had made it all the way to California, was arrested in 1941 and jailed in the States before being transferred back to Oakalla.

An eight-hour standoff in 1990 sounded the final death knell for the facility (by now called the Lower Mainland Regional Correctional Centre), and the following year, the doors were slammed shut for good. In 1992, the wreckers moved in. What replaced the largely unlamented prison complex was a townhouse complex of more than five hundred units with scenic views of Deer Lake and the North Shore mountains.

Final victory to the NIMBYists.

A forbidding stone face frowns down on you as you climb the stairs to the great front doors of the Don Jail. Father Time is watching you. Enough to give you a guilty conscience, if you don't already have one. Says former Don custodian Paul McMaster, "Someone coined the phrase years ago 'Every man that walks through these doors, walks through time.'"

But time has not been kind to these institutions, all launched with great fanfare as state-of-the-art architectural wonders based on forward-looking reformist penal principles. All ended up being described as "monstrous relics," or "black cesspools," or worse.

Carleton County Gaol has fared the best. It remains a vibrant con-cern, still accommodating "inmates." Today, people happily pay to cram themselves into the narrow, uncomfortable cells for the night. You can even take a tour around the facility and walk in Patrick Whelan's footsteps along the short passage from death row to the execution chamber, where a noose still dangles.

By the 2000s, all that remained of Oakalla was a stone marker and a flight of old stone steps leading nowhere.

The Don building now serves as the administrative centre for the new Bridgepoint Health centre, which opened in 2013. The former latrine that served as the execution chamber is firmly under lock and key. If you do manage to gain access to the room, you'll see that both the cross beam that supported the rope and the platform and trap door have been removed. The gallows, too, are gone. To the horror of civic leaders, the general public, the City of Toronto's historical board, and, presumably, some dedicated souvenir hunters, the gallows were secretly dismantled and destroyed on the orders of Ontario Correctional Services Minister Frank Drea in December 1977. But etched into the walls of the chamber are the ghostly grey geometric shapes that still mark the position where the wood and steel structure once stood.

CHAPTER 16

The End of the Rope

Both long before Confederation and after, jostling and jeering crowds gathered in their hundreds and even thousands to witness the spectacle of public executions. When Joseph Ruel was hanged at St-Hyacinthe on Dominion Day, 1868, more than eight thousand men, women, and children encircled the scaffold to watch him die. In 1881, a drunk and disorderly mob battered down the fence of the Annapolis County jail to get a really close look at Joseph Thibeau's last moments. Dozens fought for perches to witness the execution of Reginald Birchall in Woodstock in 1890, and in 1954, a mob of teenagers joked and set off firecrackers when Peter Balcombe met his end in Cornwall.

But the crowd at the piercingly cold corner of Don Jail Roadway and Gerrard Street East in Toronto on the night of December 10, 1962, was different. They were circling to protest the imminent hangings of Ronald Turpin and Arthur Lucas. There were just fifteen picketers in all, waving signs scrawled with slogans like CAPITAL PUNISHMENT IS NO DETERRENT and THOU SHALT NOT KILL.

A small group, to be sure, but a significant token of societal shift.

"I hope to make people aware of the fact that men are dying merely for vengeance," one woman told a CBC reporter.

The question of capital punishment has always stirred up strong and ambivalent feelings.

Remember farmer and premier Ernest Charles Drury, who spent twenty-five years as the sheriff of Simcoe County?

> I am opposed to capital punishment, but not for senti-
> mental reasons — though the one execution which I
> did witness was, God knows, horrible enough. I do not
> believe that capital punishment serves the cause of justice.
> Justice should be impersonal. The death penalty intro-
> duces highly emotional elements which judge and jury,
> being human, cannot disregard. Then too there is always
> the doubt. Unquestionably, innocent men have been exe-
> cuted, just as guilty men have been set free. Further, there
> is the effect on the public mind: I cannot forget that eager
> crowd gathered outside the jail, to peek [at an execution
> through cracks in a wall], after the late movies.
>
> Would not the cause of justice be better served if the
> penalty were not death but real life imprisonment, with
> no reprieve, but with always the opportunity to correct
> a mistake, if a mistake has been made?

Drury proved himself to be truly human with his own knee-jerk and highly emotional reaction to a face-to-face encounter with the hangman: "Execution was set for shortly before Christmas, and some ten days in advance a man presented himself in my office. He told me his name, but he did not need to. I knew, and the name sent a chill down my spine. I did not shake hands."

As pointed out by David B. Chandler in *Capital Punishment in Canada,* the first attempt to abolish the death penalty in Canada dates back to 1914, when Liberal Member of Parliament (MP) Robert Bickerdike submitted a private member's bill to parliament. You could say that Bickerdike was not exactly a fan of capital punishment. To illustrate, here is a selection of his comments made during the debate as published in *The Globe* in February 1914. "Capital punishment," he declared, "is a blot on Christianity and a blight on religion." It did not act as a crime deterrent; it was simply vengeance. "From judge to hangman," those concerned were guilty of "brutalized, legal murder." And his opinion on paying the hangman for his services? "Think of a government making a contract at so much per head for sending its fellow citizens into eternity, and giving him a bonus of thirty pieces of silver if he makes a good job of it!"

His passionate arguments had not the slightest effect, and his bill was defeated. Bickerdike was mightily persistent, and he tried again in 1915, 1916, and 1917. Again, no success, although he did provoke some angry pushback from people who, unlike him, believed that the death sentence had to be retained. During one of those parliamentary debates, for example, Minister of Justice Charles Doherty raised the spectre of brutish foreigners to explain a spike in the murder rate: "We are getting flooded with a population who are accustomed to think that you can kill your neighbour but that your life is so sacred that the state will never touch you."

After a long drought between the two world wars, private member's bills against capital punishment were again introduced in the early 1950s, and, again, they were defeated. Then in December 1953, Minister of Justice Stuart Garson appointed a special joint committee of the House and Senate to study, weird as the combination sounds, "capital punishment, corporal punishment, and lotteries." The committee reported back in 1956, with a recommendation to retain the death penalty, except for children younger than eighteen years.

The report went nowhere. It would take extensive political will to push through the abolition of capital punishment, but nobody was sufficiently fired up as yet. As Arthur Maloney, who was a Conservative MP as well as a renowned criminal lawyer, said during a parliamentary debate in May 1961: "What the people who favour abolition, who sincerely believe in the wisdom of abolition, have to do is to create in the public an awareness of the futility of the penalty of death."

But in truth it was not just a handful of lonely backbenchers who were interested in bringing about changes to the criminal justice system in mid-twentieth-century Canada. In addition to Maloney, for example, another powerful politician jumped onto the abolitionist bandwagon — Liberal Party leader Lester B. Pearson. To illustrate, this lively 1967 exchange between Pearson (by then prime minister) and a House of Commons "chorus," as quoted by Joel Kropf in *A Matter of Deep Personal Conscience*:

> Mr. Pearson: I believe the only logical explanation left for retaining capital punishment in our society is a desire for retaliation —
> Some hon. Members: No, no.
> Mr. Pearson: — and for revenge.
> Some hon. Members: No, no.
> Mr. Pearson: It is to make the punishment fit the crime.
> Some hon. Members: No, no.
> Mr. Pearson: The criminal kills, so he must be killed.
> Some hon. Members: No, no.
> Mr. Pearson: Well, Mr. Speaker, I cannot believe that this is an adequate reason in any society that aspires to become truly civilized.

However, you could hardly find a more passionate opponent of the death sentence than the man who became the thirteenth prime minister of Canada in 1957, Conservative John George Diefenbaker.

Diefenbaker, or Dief, as he was affectionately called, was born in Ontario in 1895, but his family moved west to Saskatchewan in 1903. When he was nine years old, Dief announced to his mother that he was going to be prime minister of Canada when he grew up. She did not laugh, and he spent the next fifty-plus years prepping himself for the job.

After a stint in the military during the First World War, Dief took the first big step along his chosen career path — he graduated as a lawyer in 1919 and started to practise criminal law. Tall and slim with piercing blue eyes and always impeccably dressed, Dief proved to be a formidable adversary in court. As mentioned by Arthur Slade in *John Diefenbaker: An Appointment with Destiny*, even hardened RCMP officers wilted under his rapid-pace cross-examinations, booming voice, and pointing, accusatory finger.

In the 1930s, Dief defended six murder cases in Prince Albert, Saskatchewan. The second of these was forever seared into his brain. His client was Alex Wysochan, a Polish immigrant enmeshed in an affair with a married woman, Antena Kropa. The couple tried to run away together, but Kropa's husband, Stanley, found them and forced them to return. A short while later, Christmas Day 1929 ushered in a deadly twist to the tale. An altercation between the two men at Kropa's house ended with the shooting death of Antena. Wysochan, found drunk by her side, was charged with murder and brought to trial in March 1930.

Slade notes that the men had wildly conflicting stories. Kropa, the star witness for the prosecution, claimed that an intoxicated Wysochan broke into their home, threatening to shoot him. Kropa leaped out the window to escape, after which he heard the shots that killed his wife. Wysochan, through a Polish interpreter, testified that Kropa found him drinking at a hotel, invited him to his house, and started a fight. Kropa pulled out a gun and shot his wife when she tried to intercede. Thereupon, Wysochan fell into a drunken stupor.

John Diefenbaker as a new Member of Parliament, May 1940. Diefenbaker was passionately opposed to capital punishment. As prime minister of Canada from 1957 to 1963, he commuted fifty-two of sixty-six death sentences.

Suffering from a gastric ulcer that confined him to bed at times during the trial, Diefenbaker was far below par. But it probably wouldn't have made much difference even if he had been at the top of his game. The prosecutor referred to Wysochan as a "reptile," a "rat," and a "dirty little coward." The jurymen, all British in origin, were repulsed by this boozy, adulterous foreigner. The judge was hostile, suspecting Wysochan of faking his need for an interpreter. The jury returned a guilty verdict, and despite Diefenbaker's appeal against the sentence, Wysochan was hanged in Prince Albert on June 20, 1930.

Diefenbaker had this to say in the House of Commons in May 1972:

> Some wonder why I have such a feeling of concern over the imposition of the death penalty. I ask those who wonder how would you feel if you defended a man charged with murder, who was as innocent as any hon. member in this House at this very moment, who was convicted; whose appeal was dismissed, who was executed; and six months later the star witness for the Crown admitted that he, himself, had committed the murder and blamed it on the accused? That experience will never be effaced from my memory.

During his term as prime minister of Canada, from 1957 to 1963, Diefenbaker commuted fifty-two of sixty-six death sentences. One of these commutations, and possibly the most significant, was that of fourteen-year-old Steven Truscott in 1960. Initially the public was exceptionally antagonistic toward Truscott, who was branded a juvenile monster. After all, they insisted, he wouldn't have been convicted unless he was guilty. Still, the optics of a boy languishing on death row were not good.

In 1961, legislation was passed to reclassify murder into two categories. Capital murder was defined as planned or intentional murder, murder that occurred during another violent crime, or the murder of an on-duty police or correctional officer. Only this type of murder would warrant the death sentence. All other murder was classified as non-capital.

Another game changer in the 1950s and 1960s was the pioneering role played by investigative journalists, a new breed of feisty reporters who made it their business to probe cases for the possibility of wrongful convictions. John Edward Belliveau and Jacques Hébert both wrote books challenging the conviction and execution of Wilbert Coffin for the 1953 slaying of bear hunter Richard Lindsey in Quebec. In her comprehensive series of articles published in the *Globe and Mail* in 1963 (called "MURDER?"), Betty Lee presented a damning exposé of the case against Arthur Lucas, recently hanged in Toronto. And Isabel LeBourdais meticulously investigated the Truscott case. Her book, which came out in 1966, turned the tide of public opinion in Truscott's favour, although it would take him another forty-one years to be finally acquitted.

Diefenbaker's Conservative government fell in 1963, and the Liberals took control. Under Pearson's leadership, the new government came out staunchly against capital punishment. Not another hanging took place, and, over the next five years, a total of forty-four death sentences were commuted.

Public reaction was mixed. In a 1966 CBC television broadcast, one interviewee said that "if a person takes a life, I think that their life should be taken in return." Another disagreed: "They shouldn't hang people at all."

But generally, the position of the public in the 1960s was firmly in favour of retaining capital punishment. As Chandler points out, "In the mid-60's, there was stable approval of the death penalty at between 50 and 58 per cent of Canadians and stable disapproval of it, between 33 and 40 per cent. A period of instability in the late 60's seemed to generate an increase in support of the death penalty to between 60 and 66 per cent of Canadians and a lessening of abolitionist opinion to 27–33 per cent."

Bucking the trend of majority opinion, the government suspended the death penalty for murder in 1967 for a trial period of five years, except for capital crimes, now redefined as cases where the victim was a police or prison officer killed in the line of duty. In 1973, this moratorium was extended for another five years.

But the history of hanging in Canada had not yet reached its final chapter. The retentionists fought back.

In July 1975, sixty-five hundred prison workers walked off the job. They demanded that capital punishment should be strictly enforced for killers of police and correctional officers. And what exactly would this achieve? "Protection," barked Paul Gascon of the Public Service Alliance of Canada in a CBC radio interview.

Abolitionist heavyweights shot back. In a CBC television interview that same year, John Diefenbaker said of the death penalty: "It's too dangerous, and innocent men can be executed and have been executed."

As the countdown continued to July 14, 1976 — the date when parliament would take a formal vote to retain or abolish the death penalty — there was still no clear indication as to which way the decision would swing. Parliamentarians would have a "free vote," meaning that they could go with their conscience. One week beforehand, another prominent politician took centre stage with a passionate speech in the House of Commons — the then Liberal prime minister, Pierre Elliott Trudeau.

"My primary concern here is not compassion for the murderer," he said. "My concern is for the society which adopts vengeance as an acceptable motive for its collective behaviour. If we make that choice, we will snuff out some of the boundless hope and confidence in ourselves and other people, which has marked our maturing as a free people."

A murder case that stoked the flames in this heated public debate on capital punishment was that of Montrealer René Vaillancourt, referred to by the *Globe and Mail* as a "bland loner" and a "cold fish." He was convicted in September 1973 for the shooting death of Constable Leslie Maitland.

Vaillancourt's early life had been marked with petty crimes such as shoplifting and auto theft. He was out on bail in February 1973 when he decided to pay a visit to Toronto and rob a bank. As he sped away after the robbery, he was pursued by Maitland and an unarmed police trainee.

"That first cop didn't want to give me his gun — that is why I shot him," said Vaillancourt: four times — first in the chest and then in the back as Maitland fell to the ground.

"I chased the other policeman trying to shoot him. He didn't have a gun out. I got in the car and shot at him from inside the car." Trainee Brian McCullum was lucky. Four bullets missed their target.

Retentionists argued that hanging the perpetrator was the only penalty appropriate for such a cold and calculated murder. Abolitionists used the case to support their cause, pointing out that Maitland himself had strongly believed that capital punishment should go for good. At the parliamentary debate on the abolition bill in July 1976, solicitor general and human rights activist Warren Allmand read from a letter by Maitland's widow pleading for Vaillancourt's life to be spared.

On July 14, Bill C-84 squeaked through, with 131 for and 124 against abolishing the death penalty for all civilian crimes. Henceforth, the punishment for first-degree (previously capital) murder would be life imprisonment without the possibility of parole for twenty-five years. The one exception was under the *National Defence Act*, where the death penalty remained in force until 1998. It was never used.

In 1987, a vigorous campaign was launched for the return of capital punishment.

"Bring it back!" urged Conservative MP Mary Collins of British Columbia in a radio interview in April of that year. She told the CBC's Peter Gzowski that on the basis of a poll and letters received, her constituents were "strongly in favour of restoring capital punishment," with a ratio of 70 percent for and 30 percent against. Did she believe that capital punishment had a deterrent effect on serious crimes? Well, that was up in the air, but "there are situations which are so horrendous that there seems to be no redeeming value in keeping the criminal in jail for the rest of his or her life." And in these cases, insisted Collins, there is a sense of justice that the criminal should be put to death.

Veteran Toronto-based defence attorney Edward Greenspan crisscrossed the country to whip up support for the anti-restoration brigade. "There is no scientific evidence that capital punishment stops murders and common sense leads to the same conclusion," he wrote in the *Toronto Star* in March 1987. "The largest number of homicides are crimes of passion. Such killings are the result of primal emotions so deep that the fear of death has not the slightest chance of restraining them.… Let us eliminate the death penalty forever from our law, and devote our energy instead to finding real, effective, but humane answers to the problem of crime."

A motion to restore the death sentence was introduced in the House of Commons on June 30. The result, again, had been difficult to predict, but this time the motion was convincingly defeated in a free vote by 148 to 127. This was a "reaffirmation vote," which would make it twice as difficult ever to reinstate the death penalty in the future.

"It's over now," said Greenspan.

CHAPTER 17

Beyond Death Row

For a hundred-plus years, from Confederation to abolition, just over half the 1,533 inmates on death row dodged the noose. They generally owed their rescue to being acquitted or offered new trials, or having their sentences reduced or their convictions quashed.

Most of them, but not all.

Some escaped simply by escaping. Most sensationally, members of the Boyd Gang broke free from the Don Jail not once but twice in the early 1950s. In 1952, they made their second escape by sawing through the bars of a window and wriggling out. They then dropped onto a fifteen-foot high wall in the exercise yard, made their way along it to the outer wall of the jail, and disappeared. On their recapture, gang leader Edwin Alonzo Boyd and member Willie Jackson were sentenced to long terms in the Kingston Penitentiary. For Lennie Jackson and Steve Suchan, the outcome was far more sinister. They had made the fatal mistake of shooting Detective Sergeant Edmund Tong while on the lam. After being found guilty of murder, they were executed in a double hanging in December 1952.

There were other, more chilling, jailbreak tactics. Witness the case of Tony Legato in 1916. George Verne of Alice Street, Guelph, Ontario, was described in 1915 as "a peaceable and respected Italian" by the *Acton*

Lennie Jackson and Steve Suchan were members of the Boyd Gang, who escaped twice from the Don Jail. After their second recapture in September 1952, the two men were sentenced to death and hanged for the murder of a policeman.

Free Press. So maybe he shouldn't have tangled with fellow immigrant Tony Legato, who, according to one source, had ties to the Italian mafia. During a confrontation, Verne slapped Legato across the face and sent him packing. Legato's answer was to return with a double-barrelled shotgun and blast Verne to eternity. Legato was eventually tracked down in Chatham, Ontario, tried for murder, and found guilty with no recommendation for mercy. His hanging was scheduled for July 5, 1916. On July 3, he spent the day peering out the window of his cell at workmen erecting the scaffold in the yard of the Guelph County Gaol. At 3:00 a.m. the following day, Legato cut his throat with the handle of a tin cup and choked himself to death with strips of his own underwear. Between 1879 and 1954, at least eight other condemned men preferred to take their own lives rather than die at the hand of the executioner.

By 1963, however, when hangman John Ellis started coiling up his ropes and preparing to spend his sunset years in Florida or the Bahamas, death row was no longer an automatic conduit to the gallows for condemned prisoners.

Take the case of the inmate they called "The Kid."

"They," as pointed out by author Robert Hoshowsky, were Arthur Lucas and Ronald Turpin, and The Kid was Gary Alexander McCorkell. Shy, vulnerable, and reportedly of limited intelligence, he, like them, was awaiting execution at the Don Jail in 1962. McCorkell was just nineteen years old. Isolated in their small cells on death row, the two older men never actually met the teenager face to face. They knew about him, though, and were greatly concerned about The Kid's physical and emotional well-being as they waited for their own appeals to wend their unsuccessful way through the criminal justice system. Deeply disturbed when Lucas and Turpin went to the gallows in December, McCorkell then had the dubious honour of moving into the newly vacated Cell Number One on death row.

Readers of the *Globe and Mail* on Apr 21, 1962, learned that McCorkell was the eldest son of a single mother. He had two siblings: an eighteen-year-old sister and a brother of sixteen. He worked as a shipper for Robert's Furniture Ltd. in New Toronto (now folded into Etobicoke), and most of his $55-a-week salary went to help his family. According to his mother, Gary liked music, movies, and roller skating, and from the age of nine, he had played cornet and horn with the Long Branch Salvation Army. Gary was never a very healthy kid, she added. He had suffered constantly from bronchial disorders and nearly died from recurrent kidney infections. What his mom did not say was that, in addition to those serious ailments, his childhood had been plagued with sexual abuse — at the age of four, he was so viciously assaulted by an older boy that he needed medical treatment and was in agony for days.

According to the *Globe and Mail*, on the morning of April 18, 1962, McCorkell's boss, Robert Rotenberg, combed through the warehouse in search of his teenaged employee, fearing that he had been injured by falling furniture. Stock clerk Jack Taniwa joined in the hunt and made several fruitless phone calls in an attempt to track McCorkell down. Morning stretched into afternoon, but the youth was nowhere to be found.

As the police revealed during their investigations into his crime, McCorkell was hiding close by. He had spotted two children, Ronald MacLeod, three, and Michael Atkinson, two, playing alone in a parking lot adjacent to the warehouse and had lured them into the building. The boys started to wail when they heard the searchers approaching. McCorkell panicked.

"I put my hand over their mouths to stop them from crying. When I let them go, I thought they were unconscious," he said in a statement to the head of Toronto's homicide squad. "I didn't realize I was going to kill them. It was an accident." He admitted, though, that prior to this, he had tied the boys' hands behind their backs and sexually molested them. He tried to revive the "unconscious" toddlers with wet cloths and smelling salts. When that failed, he walked over to the nearby Lake Shore Hospital for help. An orderly went back to the warehouse with him. Just one glance at their small, still bodies was all it took for the medic to determine that both boys were dead. He called the police.

The molested had become the molester. By the time he went on trial in October 1962 for the capital murder of Ronald MacLeod, McCorkell had a record stretching back seven years or so of sexual attacks on younger boys. Clinically classified as a homosexual pedophile, he had been receiving psychiatric treatment.

The Crown set out to prove that the toddlers had been tied up, sexually assaulted, and smothered. McCorkell, described by the *Toronto Star* as "tall, slender and pale-faced with dark wavy hair," sat quietly, staring straight ahead, as the evidence piled up against him. A pathologist confirmed that the cause of death was suffocation. A psychiatrist testified that McCorkell was not mentally ill when he committed the crime.

Leading McCorkell's defence team was one of the heaviest hitters of the day, Arthur Maloney — the same lawyer who had conducted the appeals against Wilbert Coffin's death sentence in Quebec in the mid-1950s. As noted by Maloney's biographer, Charles Pullen, Maloney had a reputation for championing the poor and the troubled, often without pay, and he readily agreed to take on the case of this penniless, intellectually challenged, working-class boy. McCorkell, argued Maloney in his address to the jury, claimed the deaths were accidental. Was this a case of capital murder? "You have got to satisfy yourself that you are satisfied beyond a reasonable doubt that the stoppage of the breath was for one of two very definite purposes: that is, that the stoppage of the breath was for the purpose of facilitating the commission of the offence of indecent assault or for the purpose of facilitating his flight after committing or attempting to commit the offence of indecent assault."

Maloney lost the battle. Although the jury recommended mercy "in the strongest possible terms," his client was sentenced to hang in February 1963.

In early 1963, Maloney took the case to the Ontario Court of Appeal. Again, he claimed that the death was only capital murder if the Crown could prove beyond a reasonable doubt that during the assault, McCorkell had plugged the mouth of his three-year-old victim to facilitate either the commission of the crime or his flight after committing it. The court, again, was not buying this argument. The appeal was dismissed, and the clock ticked inexorably toward February 26, the day McCorkell was to hang.

Fortunately for McCorkell, he had another exceptionally heavy hitter on his team — Salvation Army chaplain Cyril Everitt, his spiritual advisor at the Don Jail and the man who had passionately but unsuccessfully supported Turpin and Lucas to the bitter end. Everitt adopted a two-pronged approach: "It's my policy, and I think it should be the policy of all spiritual advisors, to do the best for the body as well as the soul of these people," he told reporters on February 23. In addition to praying for the young man, Everitt vigorously petitioned both Justice Minister Donald Fleming and Prime Minister John Diefenbaker on McCorkell's behalf. Impossible to resist: the death sentence was commuted to life imprisonment.

When the federal Liberals swept Team Diefenbaker out of office in 1963, they immediately put the kibosh on hanging by commuting every death sentence that came their way. This was made official in December 1967, when parliament voted to suspend the death penalty for a five-year trial period. The definition of a capital crime was significantly narrowed, now restricted to murders where the victim was a police or correctional officer killed while on duty. As reported in the *Montreal Gazette* in January 1968, sixteen men (twelve in Quebec, two in Ontario, and two in British Columbia) were awaiting the hangman's noose for what had now become non-capital crimes. All of these outstanding death sentences were commuted by the federal Cabinet, bringing the number of commutations issued by the Liberal government to forty-four.

The next major step on the path to abolition came in 1973, with a thirteen-vote majority in parliament extending the moratorium on capital punishment for another five years. More nail-biting for the abolitionists, until their final success in July 1976; in that oh-so-close free vote, Bill C-84 was passed. The death penalty was abolished at last for all civilian crimes.

At that time, there were eleven hard-core male prisoners, the so-called "Lucky Eleven," awaiting their fate on death row for capital murders. Eight of them had been sentenced to death for killing police officers, and three for killing correctional officials.

One of the particularly egregious police killers was Elery Steven Long. He already had a long list of criminal activities on his slate when he scored the death penalty for killing Police Staff Sergeant Ron McKay of Delta, British Columbia. McKay was following up on a disturbance at a gas station in November 1974 when he knocked at Long's front door, to be greeted with a fatal shotgun blast to the chest. Long fled but turned himself in some hours later, accompanied by his lawyer. At his trial, the jury was impervious to his claim that he had been drunk and did not remember shooting the policeman. They made no request for clemency.

The Lucky Eleven also included an exceedingly villainous duo who were locked up on death row in Moncton, New Brunswick: Richard Ambrose and James Hutchinson. Their crime spree began with the kidnapping of a teenager, Raymond Stein, who was snatched from his home by two armed and hooded men just before midnight on Thursday, December 12, 1974. The fourteen-year-old was released unharmed after a ransom of $15,000 was paid by his father, who owned a local seafood restaurant.

Under the grim headline "MONCTON POLICEMEN MURDERED: Bodies found in shallow graves," the *Halifax Chronicle-Herald* of

Monday, December 16, 1974, announced the news that everyone had been dreading ever since police had seized a motor vehicle the previous Saturday and arrested a suspect in the kidnapping. Ominously, they had found a pair of bloodied gloves in the car. The two slain officers, Corporal Aurèle Bourgeois and Constable Michael O'Leary, had both been working on the case. They had radioed in early Friday morning to say they were investigating a suspicious-looking car. That was the last anyone heard from them.

The bodies of Bourgeois and O'Leary, both married men with families, were discovered in a wooded area about fifteen miles from the city. "The two were found buried in shallow graves Sunday, shot through the head and wearing handcuffs," reported the *Chronicle-Herald* sombrely.

One of the kidnappers-turned-murderers, twenty-six-year-old Richard Ambrose, was already in custody. He was the man found in the car along with the blood-stained gloves. The hunt for his partner in crime, James Hutchinson, aged forty-seven and considered by the police to be "armed and extremely dangerous," stretched on until Sunday evening, when Hutchinson was finally arrested in a Moncton apartment building.

Both men were sentenced to hang for the murders. No mercy recommendations for them.

Three other members of the Lucky Eleven were sitting on death row for murdering correctional officers. Former Vancouver newsman Georges Joseph Péloquin was one of them. In July 1974, he was serving a sentence for armed robbery at Stony Mountain Penitentiary in Manitoba when he attacked a carpentry instructor, Stanley Green, with a metal clamp. Green later died in hospital. According to the *Globe and Mail* in March 1975, Péloquin's former wife stated at his trial that the pressures of his job as a television reporter drove him to drugs, and a prison psychiatrist testified that Péloquin believed at the time of the murder that he was being persecuted by prison officials. In spite of an eleven-page confession, the jury still made a recommendation for mercy.

The second of the prison guard killers was Gilles Hébert. He was serving a twenty-five-year sentence for armed robbery in Montreal in June 1975 when he retrieved a hidden weapon and shot two penitentiary guards who had escorted him to hospital for stomach X-rays. Paul

Gosselin died; Robert Gravel survived; Hébert escaped. On his recapture two months later, he was tried and sentenced to death.

And in April 1975, the very last man to land on death row, Mario Gauthier, killed Georges Nadeau, the chief paint shop instructor at Cowansville Penitentiary in Quebec, with multiple hammer blows to the head. At the time of the attack, the *Globe and Mail* reported, the drug-fuelled Gauthier had just eighteen days of his original sentence remaining. At his subsequent trial, the jury of seven men and five women — a very rare configuration in a system that had traditionally been the domain of men alone — deliberated for less than an hour before rejecting a defence plea of temporary insanity and returning a verdict of guilty with no request for clemency.

After July 1976, the maximum sentence for first-degree (previously capital) murder became life imprisonment, with no chance of parole for twenty-five years. All eleven death row occupants were transferred from local or provincial prisons to serve out their life sentences in federal penitentiaries. "Parole years away for 11 murderers," reported the *Globe and Mail* in February 1977. "First-degree killers can't expect to be released until turn of century." At that point, all of them were "serving their time in windowless concrete cells with steel doors." Hardly first-class accommodation, to be sure.

Eleven men; eleven commutations. And the Department of Justice case files for the Lucky Eleven were all stamped with the words "Abolishment of death penalty" to explain their getaway from death row.

CHAPTER 18

Britain Heads Toward Abolition

Canada has Britain to thank for its criminal justice system, which all stemmed from a Royal Proclamation in 1763 imposing English law on Britain's North American colonies. The British freely exported hanging to their network of dominions, colonies, protectorates, mandates, and other territories scattered around the world. And while Canada struggled to navigate the rocky passage toward the abolition of capital punishment, the mother ship was plying her own difficult course. For once, Canada got there first — 1962 marked the de facto end of hangings in the country.

Britain lagged behind. Three executions took place in England in 1962 and three the following year in Scotland and England. Also, there was a great deal of public support for capital punishment at the time. (There still is, in fact — as recently as 2010, 51 percent of those surveyed in a poll were in favour of reinstating the death penalty in Britain; 37 percent were opposed.)

And then in 1964 came the murder of John Alan West, a fifty-three-year-old driver for the Lakeland Laundry in Workington, Cumberland.

As noted by Elwyn Jones in *The Last Two to Hang*, Mary Allen of Preston, Lancashire, called the local branch of the Royal Society for the Prevention of Cruelty to Animals on Tuesday evening, April 7, 1964, and asked for an inspector to come around to her house and collect a little lamb. Inspector Nairn was pleased to oblige. He was met by Mrs. Allen, her husband, and another man, who seemed to be a lodger. They had been out for a drive that day, Mrs. Allen explained, and had found the animal on the moors between Liverpool and Clitheroe. They were all very concerned because they couldn't get it to eat properly.

What the trio neglected to tell the inspector was that they had two small children with them at the time, and that they had been speeding home in a stolen black Ford Prefect, registration number NXC 771. The car was reported to the police that same Tuesday evening as having been suspiciously abandoned in a builders' yard in Ormskirk, Lancashire.

Mary's husband, Peter Anthony Allen, and their lodger, Gwynne Owen Evans, had packed Mary and the kids into the car and gone to Seaton, Cumberland, on Monday evening, April 6. Their plan was to visit Evans's former co-worker, John (also known as Jack) Alan West.

As Evans later told the police: "Jack West has been a friend of mine for five years and he told me that if I was ever short of money he would always lend me a couple of quid. I knew he had a load of cash and so did Peter." And Peter Allen was desperately in need of hard cash to pay a fine and the rates on his house.

The group arrived at its destination in the early morning of Tuesday, April 7. Evans went to the door alone, finding West up and nursing a headache.

At around 3:00 a.m., West's next-door neighbour, Joseph Hardon Fawcett, was awakened by what he later described as "heavy thuds, as though something was hitting the foundation of the house," and he seemed to "recollect a shrill scream" coming from next door. Fawcett got out of bed, just in time to hear a car engine starting up and to see the rear lights of a vehicle as it raced away.

He and another neighbour called the police, who were on the scene by 3:45 a.m. "I saw the body of a man lying on the floor at the foot of the stairs," reported Sergeant James William Park. "There were obvious severe head injuries. There was a large amount of blood on the floor, and the man was obviously dead … it appeared that a struggle had taken place." The body was that of Jack West, stabbed and bludgeoned to death.

Less than forty-eight hours later, the killers were in custody. One of them had thoughtfully left a raincoat hanging neatly over a chair in West's bedroom, with a treasure trove of identifying items in the pockets. Among them was a medallion with the name G.O. Evans inscribed on the back. Scribbled on an army memorandum form was another useful clue — the name and address of a Liverpool woman, Norma O'Brien. O'Brien recognized the medallion and was happy to furnish the police with details of its owner, a man calling himself "Ginger" Owen Evans, whom she had met in Preston the previous year.

As with a child's puzzle, the police just had to follow the dots to find the culprits. One by one, they pulled in Allen, then his wife, and lastly Evans. Both men were well known to police, both with a history of convictions for minor crimes. The duo's spoils this time? The princely sum of ten pounds withdrawn from West's bank account using his stolen bank books, and West's gold watch, which Evans had grabbed on his way out of the house.

As West was killed in the course of a theft, Allen and Evans were both charged with capital murder under the *Homicide Act* of 1957. They were tried jointly in Manchester on June 23, 1964, with Mary Allen testifying in her husband's defence.

The two men's stories differed wildly.

Allen said that Evans was the first to enter West's house. Subsequently, Evans came out and invited him (Allen) in. While on his way upstairs, Allen was startled by West and hit him just a very few times. Evans wielded the knife and did most of the damage.

Evans claimed that he was not involved in the murder at all. His intention had been to borrow money from West, not to rob him (Jack "was like a father to me"), and certainly not to kill him. Allen, Evans said, burst into the house uninvited and was met by West, whereupon Allen attacked him viciously. As proof, Evans pointed out that Allen's clothes were drenched in blood; his own were clean.

By all accounts, Mary Allen and her lodger had been much more than friends, but during the trial, she turned on Evans fiercely. She supported her husband's claim that Evans had come out to the car to fetch Allen, and had subsequently savagely attacked his "friend" and "father."

A huge array of circumstantial evidence undermined Evans's claims and pointed to his guilt. West was found wearing just a shirt and vest. It did not seem likely that he would have gone to the door so inappropriately dressed. His false teeth, which had been knocked out of his mouth, were found at the top of the stairs. There was also the testimony of the neighbours that the lights had come on upstairs before they came on downstairs, and the forensic evidence showing blood spots and splashes on the upstairs walls and stairs. All these details tallied with Allen's account of the affair.

Had the murder been committed by one of the men alone, with the other guilty of non-capital murder at the most? The jury didn't think so. It took just three-and-a-quarter hours for them to reach a verdict: Allen and Evans were both guilty of capital murder.

Both men appealed. Their appeals were dismissed and the date of execution set for August 13, 1964.

According to Elwyn Jones, the irony was that despite the brutality of the crime, few people expected Evans and Allen to hang. The number of hangings in Britain had dribbled down to fewer than four a year, and there had been none at all in 1964. The perpetrator of another particularly violent murder in Lancashire, Joseph Wilson Masters, had just had his sentence commuted. Masters, twenty-two, had robbed and beaten to death seventy-five-year-old James Littler in his house after the man had offered him a cup of tea.

Given that the cause of abolitionists had been gaining ground since the *Homicide Act* of 1957, even the police in the north of England expected Evans and Allen to be reprieved.

In the end, it was all very low key. No fanfare, no violent protests, no overnight vigils. And hardly a peep from the press. Typical was a terse three-paragraph report in the *Glasgow Herald* on August 14, 1964, beneath the headline "Two Executed for Murder":

> The two dairymen sentenced to death at Manchester Crown Court on July 7 for the capital murder of a van driver were executed yesterday at separate prisons.
>
> Peter Anthony Allen (21) was executed at Walton Prison, Liverpool, and Gwynne Owen Evans (24)

at Manchester [Strangeways] Prison. Both lived in Clarendon Street, Preston.

Their appeals to the Court of Criminal Appeal on July 21 were lost, Lord Parker (Lord Chief Justice) saying: — "A more brutal murder it would be difficult to imagine."

When Ronald Turpin and Arthur Lucas were hanged in Canada in December 1962, the general public was aware that theirs would probably be the very last executions in Canada. Even the condemned men knew, although they took no consolation from that fact. However, when Allen and Evans went to the gallows simultaneously (although at separate prisons) in Britain in August 1964, no one — not the murderers, nor officials in the criminal justice system, not even the government itself — knew that both literally and figuratively, this was to be the end of the rope in Britain. As in Canada, the hangman would soon be out of a job.

The abolitionists had to wait just a little bit longer — until October 1964, in fact, when the Labour government of Harold Wilson came to office. One of the new government's top priorities was the elimination of capital punishment, and after the election, the use of the death penalty was suspended. Labour MP Samuel Sydney Silverman, a passionate abolitionist for twenty-plus years, introduced a private member's bill to replace the death sentence with a mandatory sentence of life imprisonment. With government support, this resulted in the *Murder (Abolition of Death Penalty) Act* of November 1965. The act was to remain in effect for a period of five years. In December 1969, both the House of Commons and the House of Lords passed a motion abolishing capital punishment permanently.

So although nobody knew it at the time, the 1964 hangings of Allen and Evans brought down the curtain on a practice that had existed in Britain for well over a thousand years, possibly introduced by the Saxons as early as the sixth century C.E.

According to Julian B. Knowles QC in *The Abolition of the Death Penalty in the United Kingdom*, "Abolition did not come about as the result of one single event, or for one reason alone. It happened because of a combination of sustained Parliamentary campaigning; public disquiet over three controversial executions in the 1950s; botched reforms to the law of murder in the 1950s; and changing attitudes towards social and penal affairs, most of all, the acceptance by an enlightened majority of MPs that the state just ought not to be in the business of taking human life."

The early part of the twentieth century saw creeping changes to the British criminal justice system — a 1908 act provided that no child under the age of sixteen could be executed. In 1933, this age was raised to eighteen. The *Infanticide Act* of 1922 made the killing of a baby by its mother no longer a capital crime, although this had in fact not taken place since 1849. A 1931 act specifically provided that no woman should be hanged after giving birth to a child for a crime committed while she was pregnant.

The first major inroads into the entrenched system of criminal law came in 1949 with the Royal Commission on Capital Punishment. By that time, parliamentarians were starting to question the death penalty more critically, with activist Sydney Silverman taking the lead. The commission was not tasked with deciding whether the death penalty should be abolished, but with considering "whether capital punishment for murder should be limited or modified." The twelve-member group met sixty-three times over the next four years, interviewing a wide range of experts in the field — judges, prison officials, spiritual advisors, medical personnel, and Britain's hangman superstar, Albert Pierrepoint.

Pierrepoint, the third and last member of a family dynasty that included his father Henry and his Uncle Tom, was the most prolific British hangman of all time. As he modestly claimed in his memoirs, "I have attended more executions in one day than any other man in this country has done in a year, more in twelve months than any other man has done in twelve years, and more in twelve years than any other man in a lifetime, though my uncle was on the list [of British executioners] for forty years." Some say Pierrepoint executed more than 600 people during his 24 year career, although a more conservative estimate puts his total at around 430.

Albert Pierrepoint was born in Clayton, West Yorkshire, in 1905, and his childhood ambition was always to follow in the footsteps of his father and beloved uncle. He got his break in 1932, when he was interviewed

Albert Pierrepoint (standing) with his uncle Thomas. It is estimated that Albert Pierrepoint hanged between 430 and 600 people during his 24-year career as British executioner in the first half of the twentieth century. He claimed to have never bungled a hanging.

and accepted as an assistant executioner. He was promoted to chief executioner in 1941, a job that came with great opportunities for travel to faraway places. For example, among his many executions were those of more than two hundred war criminals in Germany and Austria after the Second World War. By 1946, this very lucrative part-time career enabled Pierrepoint and his wife, Annie, to purchase a pub in Manchester. He carried on working as a publican long after resigning from his position as hangman in 1956.

It was a no-brainer that Pierrepoint would be invited to offer his opinions to the Royal Commission on Capital Punishment in 1949. Unlike the Canadian hangmen whose careers were littered with multiple bumbles and bungles, Pierrepoint claimed that his track record was spotless. To commission chairperson Sir Ernest Gowers's question "I suppose you must, in so many executions, have had things go wrong occasionally?" his reply was an emphatic "Never."

The commission's report, published in 1953, ran to a whopping 506 pages. In spite of its many recommendations, the Capital Punishment UK website states that "in reality there was little significant change as a result of the Commission's painstaking and highly detailed analysis of the system of capital punishment in Britain and abroad." The bottom line was that the commission believed that execution should be clean, dignified, and rapid, and they supported the British "long drop" method as described by Pierrepoint as being the best there was.

In addition to contributing to the commission's report, Pierrepoint was a common element linking together three shocking executions in the 1950s — he was the hangman in each case. Each of them, as Knowles remarks, "raised different concerns but, taken together, they made the case for abolition in a way that purely theoretical and moral arguments could not."

The tragic tale of Timothy Evans, who was hanged in 1950, horrified the public. As the facts emerged over time, it became clear that Evans was innocent beyond any reasonable doubt of the crimes attributed to him. Evans and his wife, Beryl, had the great misfortunate of renting a flat at 10 Rillington Place, Notting Hill, London, and to have as downstairs neighbours John Reginald Halliday Christie and his wife, Ethel. Who would have guessed that the balding, bespectacled, inoffensive-looking Christie was a necrophiliac serial killer who would end up murdering at least eight women? Among his victims were Evans's wife, Beryl, and their infant daughter. Shocked by his loss and hoodwinked by the cunning Christie, Evans initially confessed to the murders. By the time he realized that Christie must have murdered the two and wanted to recant, it was too late. Evans was tried and sentenced to death in January 1950, and hanged two months later. In 1953, a new tenant at 10 Rillington Place found the bodies of three women, and further searches turned up three more, among them that of Christie's wife. After his arrest, Christie confessed to killing Beryl Evans, but a subsequent commission of inquiry ruled that his evidence was unreliable. Christie was executed for the murder of his wife (enter Pierrepoint, again), but it would take a further thirteen years before Evans was granted a posthumous pardon.

The firestorm of controversy over the possibility that an innocent man had gone to the gallows was further inflamed by the troubling execution of nineteen-year-old Derek Bentley in 1953. Bentley and a younger friend, Christopher Craig, sixteen, tried to break into a warehouse in Croydon, London, in November 1952. Craig was armed with a revolver, which he used to wound a police officer who tackled them, and to shoot dead another. Police witnesses claimed that even though Bentley was under arrest when the fatal bullet was discharged, he had earlier encouraged Craig to fire. Bentley had an IQ of seventy-seven; he had suffered brain damage as a child; he was epileptic. Nevertheless, he was judged fit to stand trial. The two youths were charged with murder, with a trial judge who greatly favoured both flogging and hanging, and both were found guilty. Craig was too young to be executed and ended up serving a prison sentence of ten years. The jury recommended mercy for Bentley. He could have escaped the noose if Home Secretary Sir David Maxwell Fyfe had exercised the royal prerogative. Instead, Fyfe ruled that "the law should take its course."

Reginald Paget QC summed up the public's outrage succinctly in parliament during an unsuccessful attempt to debate Bentley's death sentence: "A three-quarter-witted boy of nineteen is to be hanged for a murder he did not commit, and which was committed fifteen minutes after he was arrested. Can we be made to keep silent when a thing as horrible and as shocking as this is to happen?"

As the *Guardian* reported on January 28, 1953: "Crowds jostled in Whitehall last night chanting, 'Bentley must be reprieved.' Outside the House of Commons over one hundred people shouted: 'Bentley must not die.'" All in vain. At 9:00 a.m. that day Bentley was hanged by Albert Pierrepoint at Wandsworth Prison. It took until 1998 for Bentley's conviction to be quashed by the Court of Appeal.

Then there was the case of Ruth Ellis, a glamorous nightclub hostess who was hanged in 1955 for pumping five bullets at point-blank range into her abusive boyfriend. Ellis made a full confession to the police and confirmed under cross-examination at her trial that her intention had been to kill the man. But Ellis was a blond, beautiful, photogenic twenty-eight-year-old mother of two, and her case triggered widespread public protest. Thousands of people signed a petition in favour of mercy. Home Secretary Gwilym Lloyd George refused a reprieve, and Ellis was hanged on July 13 at Holloway Prison, London — the last woman ever executed in the United Kingdom.

Albert Pierrepoint, her executioner, suffered from the resultant backlash and complained bitterly about the arbitrary nature of the mercy process. Why, he wondered, had the crowds now protesting vigorously against Ellis's fate so completely ignored the plight of Styllou Christofi, a grey-haired grandmother executed just six months previously for murdering her daughter-in-law?

> When I left Holloway after the execution of Ruth Ellis, the prison was almost besieged by a storming mob. I needed police protection to get me through.... At Euston Station a crowd of newspapermen were awaiting me. I shielded my face from the cameras as I ran for my train. One young reporter jogged alongside me asking "How did it feel to hang a woman, Mr. Pierrepoint?" I did not answer. But I could have asked: "Why weren't you waiting to ask me that question last year, sonny? Wasn't Mrs. Christofi a woman, too?"

The *Homicide Act (1957)* pulled some of the teeth from the death penalty. As with a similar Canadian law passed in 1961, the new offence of capital murder was created. In Britain, this applied to murder accompanied by theft, murder by shooting or an explosion, murder in the course of resisting arrest or escaping from custody, the killing of a police or prison officer, and second murders. Had it been in force a few years earlier, this act may well have changed things for Bentley, as one of the sections provided that only the person who actually committed a murder would be liable for the death penalty. But as Liz Homans points out in her article "Swinging Sixties," both retentionists and abolitionists objected to an act they saw as clunky and unworkable. For example, why should murder after rape not be a capital crime if the victim was stabbed to death, but punishable by death if the victim was shot? As quoted by *The Telegraph* in 1964, the Lord Chief Justice described the law as a "hopeless muddle."

The tide was slowly turning against capital punishment. Abolitionists were supported by the Church and the judiciary. But bringing public opinion around was not so easy.

The *Murder (Abolition of Death Penalty) Act* of November 1965, which was to remain in effect for five years, did not bring the controversy to an end. The public reacted violently when three policemen were shot dead in London in 1966, and the Police Federation called for the recall of hanging for the crime of murdering a policeman. In a 1967 article in the *Ottawa Citizen* entitled "Bring back noose, Britons cry," Don McGillivray wrote: "Britain's five-year experiment with the complete abolition of capital punishment is two years old on Wednesday and already a petition to bring back hanging is gathering 5,000 signatures a week." It was a nail-biting battle, but in December 1969, the members of both the British House of Commons, on a free vote of 343 to 185, and the House of Lords passed a motion permanently abolishing capital punishment.

In an editorial the British *Daily Mirror* acknowledged that public opinion was against abolition. But, it added, "it must always be the duty of Parliament to lead if there is ever to be any progress in penal reform. The lead has been given. It is clear cut. It is humane. This agonising controversy can now be buried with the hangman's noose."

CONCLUSION

The game is over.

Never again, at the end of a court case in Canada, will a judge don a black cap and black gloves and utter these grim words: "Prisoner at the Bar, it becomes my painful duty to pass the final sentence of the law upon you. You have been found guilty of murder. You will be taken from here to the place whence you came and there be hanged by the neck until you are dead, and may God have mercy on your soul."

Nevermore will a prisoner languish on death row waiting for the results of an appeal, or tremble at the sound of a scaffold being constructed outside his or her cell window. Gone are the days when the press described in precise detail the forty-pace walk or the thirteen-step climb to the gallows. No longer does a black flag fly and a bell toll seven solemn times at Montreal's infamous Bordeaux jail to herald a death by hanging.

The players who took part in Canada's deadly game of Hangman — accused, policemen, sheriffs, lawyers, judges, juries, hangmen, government officials — are, for the most part, gone. And they paid the price. Many of them were in some profound way touched, twisted, or broken by their participation in the process. Some turned to alcohol or drugs to dull the pain; others broke down under the mental and emotional pressure; yet others committed suicide.

One of the foremost players died in 1985: lawyer, author, commissioner, and justice "Hanging Jim" (also known as "Vinegar Jim") McRuer. He stands out as the tough, demanding judge who presided over the trial of *Regina v. Lucas* in 1962. Was the large, slow-witted Arthur Lucas actually guilty of the gangland-style killing of Therland Crater? Should Lucas have been hanged? Controversy lingers to this day.

Hanging Jim's biographer, Patrick Boyer, writes that although the judge showed a certain readiness to sentence murderers to death, his thoughts about capital punishment were not clear. When quizzed on the topic, Justice McRuer would simply say that he was doing his duty. Would he support the restoration of the death penalty post-1976? "I do not know," he replied.

In Boyer's opinion, "Given his commitment to justice, however, it seems reasonable to conclude that he viewed hanging as an appropriate punishment for a heinous crime. In short, capital punishment in his mind could be an instrument of justice, a way of ensuring that human life was respected and that no person could kill another with impunity. It was the law, in any case."

And yet, in an interview with journalist and author Jack Batten in the spring of 1985, the ninety-five-year-old McRuer pronounced his definitive legal and personal opinion on the divisive Arthur Lucas case in particular and capital punishment in general: "There was one good thing about Lucas's hanging," mused the venerable judge from his armchair. "It was the last. Parliament ended the death penalty, and sentencing a man to hang is one part of the administration of justice that judges need have no fear of now."

It was over. In a timeline stretching from 1967 through 1976 to 1987, parliament chipped away at, and finally abolished, capital punishment for civil crimes in Canada. In 1998, the country achieved full abolitionist status when the last references to the death penalty were removed from the *National Defence Act*. Although important, this was in a sense a technicality, as there had not been a military execution since 1945.

But like a dormant volcano, the issue bubbles away just beneath the surface of public consciousness, ready to erupt when something dreadful happens — something like the reign of terror in southern Ontario that ended with the trial of serial "Scarborough-rapist"-turned-killer Paul Bernardo in 1995. Or the serial murders in the 1990s and early 2000s of possibly as many as forty-nine women in Port Coquitlam, British Columbia, by pig-farmer Robert William "Willie" Pickton.

Or we can just look to the flash point that occurred fifty years after the last hanging in Canada. Victoria "Tori" Stafford was just eight years old when she was abducted from Woodstock, Ontario, in April 2009. A month later, police arrested twenty-eight-year-old Michael Thomas Rafferty, and Terri-Lynne McClintic, eighteen. On March 5, 2012, Rafferty's trial began for the kidnapping, sexual assault, and first-degree murder of the little girl. This prompted Paul Russell, letters editor of the *National Post*, to ask his readers: "Should Canada bring back the death penalty?" An avalanche of replies tumbled in.

"Yes!" said the majority. "Tori Stafford was just the latest victim of cruelty, thrust on her by the dregs of human wreckage. Like any dregs, such depraved individuals are good for nothing but compost, if that. Unhooded, disgust and contempt in my eyes, I'd be happy to put the noose around their necks and pull the trapdoor," wrote one correspondent. "The death penalty for certain crimes? Yes. And let's have those put to death then donate their organs for transplant," suggested another. Some letter writers invoked the word of God: "In direct rebuttal to those who say we can't afford the death penalty — we can't afford to continue warehousing murderers. As God Almighty commanded. Gen. 9:6: 'Whoso sheddeth man's blood, by man shall his blood be shed.' So let's bring back the noose already."

The two-wrongs-do-not-make-a-right side was horrified. "I am disgusted by my bloodthirsty, vengeance-seeking fellow citizens. Most jurisdictions have turned away from this barbaric practice. If people want to kill someone so badly, the penalty should only be applied in name of those so quick to call for death. Not in my name or my children's or the rest of this once sane and reasonable country." Another naysayer commented: "Man's propensity for error, whether in law, medicine, economics, politics, etc., is legion. We should be sufficiently humble to acknowledge our fallibilities and not allow for another source of error by revisiting capital punishment." And the word of God was brought in to bolster the argument here, too: "All life is sacred. Criminals are humans who, despite their crime, deserve to be treated with respect and dignity. God's mission is to bring salvation to all men and women. His salvation is not imposed but reaches us through acts of love, mercy and forgiveness that we can carry out."

Other letter writers adopted a more nuanced approach: "We should bring the death penalty back but not use it. Bringing it back allows retributionists to say, 'We're tough on crime.' And not applying it allows the more-enlightened-than-thou crowd to say 'Yes, we could, but we don't; aren't we just so darned morally superior?' This should keep both sides quiet for another ten years; then we can start the whole debate all over again. Or not."

One female reader offered this opinion: "We should not endorse capital punishment. Castration should be legalized as a cure and a deterrent for sexual deviants. Women have said this for years."

In 2013, a different and more structured survey of public opinion was conducted via an online Angus Reid poll. "All things considered," respondents were asked, "would you support or oppose reinstating the death penalty for murder in Canada?"

"Bring back capital punishment" was the response of 63 percent of those polled, as opposed to 30 percent who disagreed.

The death penalty would serve as a deterrent to potential murderers, argued the 63 percent in favour. It would save taxpayers tons of money; namely, the costs associated with imprisoning murderers for years on end. If you take a life, you should lose yours in return. The death penalty provides closure to the families of murder victims. And, finally, murderers cannot be rehabilitated.

Not so, argued the 30 percent opposed to capital punishment. What about wrongful conviction and the possibility of executing innocent people? Even if convicted murderers have taken a life, it is simply wrong for them to lose theirs as punishment. The death penalty is not a deterrent, and murderers should pay the price by doing time in prison, as decided by a judge. And, finally, murderers can be rehabilitated.

The results of this opinion poll were very similar to a 2012 poll, also by Angus Reid, and there is nothing to suggest that a survey conducted today would be very different.

In case you're wondering what the most prominent hangmen since Confederation might have brought to the debate: John Radclive, official executioner in the late 1800s and early 1900s, became increasingly opposed to capital punishment in his last years. Canada's most famous hangman, Arthur Ellis, was always a committed advocate of capital punishment, but, as author Frank Anderson points out, in his later years, he came out forcefully against hanging. "Hanging belongs to a past age," Ellis wrote in 1935. "I am strongly in favour of the electric chair, not only on the ground of Humanity but it is safer in every way and it is instantaneous."

A contrasting opinion was voiced by John Ellis, Canada's last executioner. He was a firm believer in capital punishment, a point of view that never changed. On the topic of opponents of hanging during his 1976 television interview with Paul Soles of the CBC, he said: "they don't realize just how humane it is. Unlike electrocution.... People want to die rather than spend life in prison."

Englishman Albert Pierrepoint, arguably the most competent hangman of all time, and certainly one of the most prolific, had this to say in his memoirs, published in 1974:

> I now sincerely hope that no man is ever called upon to carry out another execution in my country. I have come to the conclusion that executions solve nothing, and are only an antiquated relic of a primitive desire for revenge which takes the easy way and hands over the responsibility for revenge to other people.... [Capital punishment] is said to be a deterrent. I cannot agree.... All the men and women whom I have faced at that final moment convince me that in what I have done I have not prevented a single murder.

However, he backpedalled somewhat in a BBC interview in 1976: "I know I wrote that in the book, and when I wrote that in the book I honestly believed it. But since then there's been a lot more crime than there was in my time and I just can't make my mind up. They talk about bringing it back for policemen, but they never mention bringing it back for the murder of children. If they bring it back, fair enough, but bring it back for everyone. A murder is a murder."

No consensus, then, among those who lent the name of their occupation to the often fatal game of Hangman.

To sum up where we stand now: in spite of what the polls tell us, it seems unlikely that capital punishment will be reintroduced in Canada. Parliament has spoken, more than once.

And yet …

Recent world events have shown that nothing is cast in stone. Something particularly horrific — a mass murder, say, or a series of monstrous crimes — might bring the issue flashing back into public consciousness and reignite the fiery age-old debate.

So the question arises: If we *could* reinstate capital punishment — *should* we?

What's *your* verdict?

ACKNOWLEDGEMENTS

This book did not start off as a book. My first thought was to write a biographical article on Canada's most famous hangman, Arthur Ellis. As my research progressed, so did my interest in evaluating the effects of capital punishment on all those who were touched by it. My first sketches morphed into a more general history of hanging in Canada — for young people. My thanks to the editorial team at Dundurn who encouraged me to convert a book for middle readers into a work of adult non-fiction, and who so ably assisted me in bringing it to print.

Special thanks to the multi-talented Tuhin Giri for the original and very striking book cover concept, to which Dundurn designers added a touch of whimsy. Tuhin applied his editing skills to every chapter, offering me pointed suggestions and insights, and, together with Cathy Landolt, he has assisted me in threading through the intricacies of book marketing.

So many others have provided support along the way. Some of them were listeners: people like Sheryl Danilowitz, Jinks Hoffmann, and Lin Judelman, whose advice helped me to hone my story telling skills.

Then there were the readers: Catherine Rondina and the members of the #9 writing group, and Paulette Bourgeois all perused and encouraged early drafts.

A big thank you to the readers of my more-or-less-final manuscript — Carolyn Poplak, Richard Poplak and Keith Pownall. Each of them brought a distinct perspective to the book that sharpened it immeasurably. Thanks, too, to Valda Poplak, who did such sterling work on my bibliography.

I have a number of other individuals and organizations to thank — among them Bill Swan; Leah Daniels; Steven E. Silver, with his wealth of knowledge about the history of executions in Canada; Win Wahrer of Innocence Canada; Patricia Petruga of the Bridgepoint Health Science Library, who, in addition to introductions and information, took me on a personal tour of Toronto's Don Jail; the members of the Bridgepoint Communications Department who allowed me to visit restricted areas within the jail; the staff of Library and Archives Canada in Ottawa and the City of Toronto Archives, who were all unfailingly courteous and obliging. And a very special shout-out to those professionals at our city's treasure, the Toronto Public Library. Their "Book a Librarian" service was particularly helpful. I scored the assistance of not one but two specialists: Alan Walker of the Special Collections Centre and Cynthia Fisher of the Humanities and Social Sciences Department.

Finally, my very grateful thanks to my husband, Phillip Poplak, who has been both a listener and a reader, and who sustained us by cooking many, many meals while I worked my way through the book.

SELECTED BIBLIOGRAPHY

NEWSPAPERS

Acton Free Press
Border Cities Star
Brockville Monitor
Carleton Sentinel
Chronicle-Herald
Common Cause (Britain)
Courier
Daily Mail and Empire
Daily Mirror (Britain)
Detroit Post
Drummondville Spokesman
Expositor
Flesherton Advance
Guardian
Glasgow Herald
Globe and Mail (originally called *The Globe*)
Granby Leader-Mail
Hanover Post
Herald-Journal

Huron Expositor
Huron Signal
Irish Canadian
Lethbridge News
London Free Press
London Times
Markdale Standard
Miami News
Milwaukee Sentinel
Montreal Daily Mail
Montreal Gazette (also called *The Gazette*)
Morning Chronicle
National Post
New York Times
Niagara Falls Gazette
Norwalk Hour
Ottawa Citizen (also called the *Ottawa Daily Citizen*)
Ottawa Journal
Ottawa Times
Pittsburgh Post-Gazette
Pittsburgh Press
Quebec Daily Telegraph
Quebec Saturday Budget
Reading Eagle
Saskatoon Star-Phoenix
Schenectady Gazette
Southeast Missourian
St. Petersburg Times
Sunday Spartanburg Herald-Journal
Telegram
Toledo Blade
Toronto Daily Mail
Toronto Globe
Toronto Star (previously called the *Toronto Daily Star*)
Toronto Sun

Toronto World
Vancouver Sun
Winnipeg Free Press

GOVERNMENT DOCUMENTS

Capital Case Files, RG 13, Department of Justice (Canada), Library and
    Archives Canada, Ottawa
Orders-in-Council (Canada)
Statutes (Canada)
Statutes (Great Britain)

OTHER SOURCES

Anastakis, Dimitry. *Death in the Peaceable Kingdom: Canadian History
    since 1867 through Murder, Execution, Assassination, and Suicide.*
    Toronto: University of Toronto Press, 2015.
Andersen, Earl. *Hard Place to Do Time: The Story of Oakalla Prison,
    1912–1991.* New Westminster, BC: Hillpointe, 1993.
Anderson, Barrie, and Dawn Anderson. *Manufacturing Guilt: Wrongful
    Convictions in Canada.* Halifax, NS: Fernwood, 1998.
Anderson, Frank W. *Hanging in Canada: Concise History of a Controversial
    Topic.* Surrey, BC: Frontier Books, 1982.
Argyle, Ray. "Reasonable Doubts." Accessed May 4, 2016. www.canadas
    history.ca/Magazine/Online-Extension/Articles/Reasonable-Doubts.
Batten, Jack. *Judges.* Toronto: Macmillan of Canada, 1986.
Belliveau, John Edward. *The Coffin Murder Case.* Toronto: Kingswood
    House, 1956.
Boyer, J. Patrick. *A Passion for Justice: How "Vinegar Jim" McRuer
    Became Canada's Greatest Law Reformer.* Toronto: Blue Butterfly
    Books, 2008.
Boyle, Terry. *Fit to Be Tied: Ontario's Murderous Past.* Toronto: Polar Bear
    Press, 2001.

Brawn, Dale. *Practically Perfect: Killers Who Got Away with Murder — for a While*. Toronto: Dundurn Press, 2013.

Brown, Chester. *Louis Riel: A Comic-Strip Biography*. Montreal: Drawn and Quarterly, 2003.

Brown, Ron. *Behind Bars: Inside Ontario's Heritage Gaols*. Toronto: Natural Heritage Books, 2006.

Cain, Patrick. "The Agony of the Executioner." *Toronto Star*, May 20, 2007. Accessed August 16, 2014. www.thestar.com/news/insight/2007/05/20/the_agony_of_the_executioner.html.

"Capital Punishment U.K." *Capital Punishment U.K.* Accessed May 12, 2016. www.capitalpunishmentuk.org/contents.html.

CBC. *Steven Truscott: His Word Against History. The Fifth Estate*. TV documentary produced by Julian Sher and hosted by Linden MacIntyre, aired March 29, 2000.

Chandler, Ann. "The Lady & the Bootlegger." *The Beaver* 84, no. 3 (2004): 40–44.

Chandler, David B. *Capital Punishment in Canada: A Sociological Study of Repressive Law*. Toronto: McClelland & Stewart, 1976.

Downs, Art, ed. *Outlaws & Lawmen of Western Canada*. Vol. 2. Surrey, BC: Heritage House Publishing, 1996.

Drury, Ernest Charles. *Farmer Premier: Memoirs of the Honourable E.C. Drury*. Toronto: McClelland & Stewart, 1966.

Faber, Harold. *Samuel de Champlain: Explorer of Canada*. New York: Benchmark Books, 2005.

Foster, Hamar. "The Kamloops Outlaws and Commissions of Assize in Nineteenth-Century British Columbia." In *Essays in the History of Canadian Law*, edited by David H. Flaherty. Vol. 2: 308–64. Toronto: Osgoode Society, 1983.

Frigon, Sylvie. "Les représentations socio-pénales des femmes 'maricides' au Canada, 1866–1954." In *Femmes et Justice Pénale: XIXe-Xxe Siècles*, edited by Christine Bard, Frédéric Chauvaud, Michelle Perrot, and Jacques Guy Petit, 209–31. Rennes: Presses Universitaires de Rennes, 2002.

———. "Mapping Scripts and Narratives of Women Who Kill Their Husbands in Canada, 1866–1954: Inscribing the Everyday." In *Killing Women: The Visual Culture of Gender and Violence*, edited by

Annette Burfoot, Susan Lord, 9–20. Waterloo, ON: Wilfrid Laurier University Press, 2011.

Gadoury, Lorraine, and Antonio Lechasseur. *Persons Sentenced to Death in Canada, 1867–1976: An Inventory of Case Files in the Fonds of the Department of Justice*. Ottawa: National Archives of Canada, 1994. Accessed October 23, 2014. http://data2.archives.ca/pdf/pdf001/p000001052.pdf.

Gaffield, Scott M. "Justice Not Done: The Hanging of Elizabeth Workman." *Canadian Journal of Law and Society* 20, no. 1 (2005): 171–92. Accessed January 21, 2015. http://muse.jhu.edu/article/201514.

Greenspan, Edward L. "Capital Punishment: The Arguments For and Against 'The Death Penalty Is Cruel Barbarism.'" *Toronto Star*, March 25, 1987. Accessed June 19, 2008. http://proquest.umi.com.ezproxy.torontopubliclibrary.ca/pqdweb?did=472623501&sid=2&Fmt=3&clientId=1525&RQT=309&VName=PQD.

Greenwood, F. Murray, and Beverley Boissery. *Uncertain Justice: Canadian Women and Capital Punishment 1754–1953*. Toronto: Dundurn Press, 2000.

Hangman's Graveyard. Documentary. Directed by Mick Grogan and produced by Daniel Thomson. Ballinran Entertainment, 2009.

Harland-Logan, Sarah. "Steven Truscott." *Innocence Canada*. Accessed June 20, 2016. www.aidwyc.org/cases/historical/steven-truscott.

Harring, Sidney L. "The Rich Men of the Country: Canadian Law in the Land of the Copper Inuit, 1914–1930." *Ottawa Law Review* 21 (1989): 1–64.

Hendley, Nate. *Steven Truscott: Decades of Injustice*. Neustadt, ON: Five Rivers, 2012.

Homans, Liz. "Swinging Sixties: The Abolition of Capital Punishment." *History Today* 58 (2008): 43–49.

Hoshowsky, Robert J. *The Last to Die: Ronald Turpin, Arthur Lucas, and the End of Capital Punishment in Canada*. Toronto: Dundurn Press, 2007.

Iacovetta, Franca. "Napolitano (Neapolitano), Angelina," in *Dictionary of Canadian Biography*, vol. 15, University of Toronto/Université Laval, 2003–. Accessed May 15, 2016. www.biographi.ca/en/bio/napolitano_angelina_15E.html.

Jones, Elwyn. *The Last Two to Hang*. London, UK: Macmillan, 1966.

Knowles, Julian B. *The Abolition of the Death Penalty in the United Kingdom*. London, UK: Death Penalty Project, 2015.

Kropf, Joel. "A Matter of Deep Personal Conscience: The Canadian Death Penalty Debate, 1957–1976." M.A. thesis, Carleton University, 2007.

Lambert, Maude-Emmanuelle. "Sault-au-Cochon Tragedy." *The Canadian Encyclopedia*. Accessed October 23, 2016. www.thecanadian encyclopedia.ca/en/article/sault-au-cochon-tragedy.

Lebourdais, Isabel. *The Trial of Steven Truscott*. Toronto: McClelland & Stewart, 1966.

Leyton-Brown, Ken. *The Practice of Execution in Canada*. Vancouver: University of British Columbia Press, 2010.

Linder, Douglas O. "Famous Trials: Louis Riel Trial 1885." Accessed May 27, 2016. http://law2.umkc.edu/faculty/projects/ftrials/riel/riel.html.

McNicoll, Susan. *Toronto Murders: Mysteries, Crime, and Scandals*. Canmore, AB: Altitude Publishing Canada, 2005.

Melady, John. *Double Trap: The Last Public Hanging in Canada*. Toronto: Dundurn Group, 2005.

Middaugh, C. Denton. *"Life and Death of the Noose in Canada."* Accessed May 4, 2016. www.academia.edu/4315394/Life_and_Death_of_the_ Noose.

Mitchell, Tom. "'Blood with the Taint of Cain': Immigrant Labouring Children, Manitoba Politics, and the Execution of Emily Hilda Blake." *Journal of Canadian Studies* 28, no. 4 (1994): 49–71.

Ontario Cemeteries Act Site Investigation: The Old Don Jail Burial Area. Toronto: Archaeological Services, 2008.

Pacholik, Barb, and Jana G. Pruden. *Boiling Point & Cold Cases: More Saskatchewan Crime Stories*. Regina, SK: University of Regina Press, 2013.

Pelchat, Andre. "A Monstrous Plot." *Canada's History*. Accessed July 21, 2016. www.canadashistory.ca/Magazine/Online-Extension/Articles/A-Monstrous-Plot.

Pfeifer, Jeffrey E., and Kenneth Bryan Leyton-Brown. *Death by Rope: An Anthology of Canadian Executions*. Regina, SK: Vanity Press, 2007.

Pierrepoint, Albert. *Executioner: Pierrepoint*. London, UK: Harrap, 1974.

Procès de Joseph Ruel, convaincu du meurtre de Toussaint Boulet, empoisonné le 12 février 1868: condamné à être pendu le 1er juillet 1868. St. Hyacinthe, [Quebec]: Imprimé à l'atelier typographique du "Courier de St. Hyacinthe," 1868. Accessed April 13, 2016. https://archive.org/details/cihm_36072.

Procès Provencher-Boisclair. Montreal: R. Goltman. Imprimé à l'atelier typographique de "La Gazette de Sorel," 1867. Accessed December 06, 2016. https://archive.org/details/cihm_04843.

Pruden, Jana G. "Hanged: A Special Series About the History of Capital Punishment in Alberta." *Edmonton Journal*. Accessed June 05, 2016. www.edmontonjournal.com/news/hanged/index.html.

Pullen, Charles. *The Life and Times of Arthur Maloney: The Last of the Tribunes*. Toronto: Dundurn Press, 1994.

Saunders, Kenneth. *The Rectory Murder: The Mysterious Crime that Shocked Turn-of-the-Century New Brunswick*. Toronto: J. Lorimer, 1989.

Sher, Julian. *Until You Are Dead: Steven Truscott's Long Ride into History*. Toronto: A.A. Knopf Canada, 2001.

Slade, Arthur. *John Diefenbaker: An Appointment with Destiny*. Montreal: XYZ Publishing, 2001.

Smith, Denis. *Rogue Tory: The Life and Legend of John G. Diefenbaker*. Toronto: MacFarlane Walter & Ross, 1995.

Smith, Peter. *Prairie Murders: Mysteries, Crimes, and Scandals*. Canmore, AB: Altitude Publishing Canada, 2005.

Spaight, George. *The Trial of Patrick J. Whelan for the Murder of the Hon. Thos. D'Arcy McGee*. Ottawa: G.E. Desbarats, 1868.

Strange, Carolyn. "The Lottery of Death: Capital Punishment, 1867–1976." *Manitoba Law Journal* 23, no. 3 (1996): 594–619.

————. "Wounded Womanhood and Dead Men: Chivalry and the Trials of Clara Ford and Carrie Davis." In *Gender Conflicts: New Essays in Women's History*, edited by Franca Iacovetta and Mariana Valverde, 149–88. Toronto: University of Toronto Press, 1992.

Swan, Bill. *Real Justice: Fourteen and Sentenced to Death: The Story of Steven Truscott*. Toronto: Lorimer, 2012.

Taylor, Fennings. *Thos. D'Arcy McGee: Sketch of his Life and Death.* Montreal: John Lovell, 1868. *Project Gutenberg Canada.* www.gutenberg.ca/ebooks/taylorf-darcymcgee/taylorf-darcymcgee-00-e.html.

Thomas, Lewis H. "Riel, Louis (1844–85)," in *Dictionary of Canadian Biography*, vol. 11, University of Toronto/Université Laval, 2003: Accessed January 30, 2017. www.biographi.ca/en/bio/riel_louis_1844_85_11E.html.

Wilson, David A., ed. *Irish Nationalism in Canada.* Montreal: McGill-Queen's University Press, 2009.

————. *Thomas D'Arcy McGee: Vol. 2: The Extreme Moderate, 1857–1868.* Montreal: McGill-Queen's University Press, 2011.

IMAGE CREDITS

75 © Government of Canada. Reproduced with the permission of Library and Archives Canada (2016). Library and Archives Canada/ Department of Justice fonds/RG13-B-1 Vol.1409 File 47 A.

92 Top: © Government of Canada. Reproduced with the permission of Library and Archives Canada (2016). Library and Archives Canada/ Department of Justice fonds/RG13-B-1 Vol.1593 File 422. Bottom: © Government of Canada. Reproduced with the permission of Library and Archives Canada (2016).Library and Archives Canada/ Department of Justice fonds/RG13-B-1 Vol.1593 File 422.

93 © Government of Canada. Reproduced with the permission of Library and Archives Canada (2016). Library and Archives Canada/Department of Justice fonds/RG13-B-1 Vol.1593. File 422.

97 Top and Bottom: © Government of Canada. Reproduced with the permission of Library and Archives Canada (2016). Library and Archives Canada/Department of Justice fonds/RG13-C-1 Vol.1420.

105 © Government of Canada. Reproduced with the permission of Library and Archives Canada (2016). Library and Archives Canada/Department of Justice fonds/RG13-B-1 Vol.1732 File 786.

111 London Free Press collection, Western Archives, Western University, June 18, 1959.

123 © Government of Canada. Reproduced with the permission of Library and Archives Canada (2016). Library and Archives Canada/Department of Justice fonds/RG13-C-1 Vol.1695.

133 © Government of Canada. Reproduced with the permission of Library and Archives Canada (2016). Library and Archives Canada/Department of Justice fonds/RG13-B-1 Vol.1838 File 902.

136 © Government of Canada. Reproduced with the permission of Library and Archives Canada (2016). Library and Archives Canada/Department of Justice fonds/RG13 Vol. 1838, cc 902.

140 City of Toronto Archives, Fonds 1244, Item 1152.

150 Rt. Hon. John G. Diefenbaker Centre, image number JGD 263, Saskatoon, Canada.

157 City of Toronto Archives, Fonds 1266, Item 148349.

170 Wikimedia Commons.

INDEX

OF RELATED INTEREST

The Toronto Book of the Dead
Adam Bunch

If these streets could talk …

With morbid tales of war and plague, duels and executions, suicides and séances, Toronto's past is filled with stories whose endings were anything but peaceful. The Toronto Book of the Dead delves into these: From ancient First Nations burial mounds to the grisly murder of Toronto's first lighthouse keeper; from the rise and fall of the city's greatest Victorian baseball star to the final days of the world's most notorious anarchist.

Toronto has witnessed countless lives lived and lost as it grew from a muddy little frontier town into a booming metropolis of concrete and glass. The Toronto Book of the Dead tells the tale of the ever-changing city through the lives and deaths of those who made it their final resting place.

dundurn.com   dundurnpress

@dundurnpress   dundurnpress

dundurnpress   info@dundurn.com

FIND US ON NETGALLEY & GOODREADS TOO!

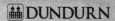
DUNDURN